D1121638

OLD DUNFERMLINE

Old Dunfermline

Mima Robertson

Paul Harris Publishing

Edinburgh and New York

First published 1979 by
Paul Harris Publishing
25 London Street
Edinburgh

ISBN 0904505 86 3

Set in Monotype Baskerville
Printed in Great Britain by
Bookmag, Henderson Road
Inverness

Contents

Paul Harris Publishing and Mima Robertson acknowledge
with grateful thanks the following for their help with this
book:

The Carnegie Dunfermline Trust

Dunfermline District Council's Director of Libraries,
Museums and Art Galleries for their permission to use
and their help in finding the old prints of Dunfermline,
pages 15, 21, 38, 39, 47, 77, 110, 117, 133, 135.

Photocraft pictures by Morris Allan, Dunfermline, pages
11, 17, 28, 53, 62, 74, 129.

Photograph by courtesy of The Dunfermline Press, back
flap.

The Scottish Arts Council for financial assistance in
publication of this volume.

1
Malcolm and Margaret

The City and Royal Burgh of Dunfermline stands, like Rome, upon several hills of varying steepness. It faces south looking over the rolling Fife countryside to the Firth of Forth, the Pentland hills and, far off to the east, the Castle Rock of Edinburgh. Dunfermline, too, has its skyline, dominated by the towers of the ancient Abbey, the clock tower of the Townhouse and the dark clustered trees of Pittencrieff Glen, clearly seen by those who approach the town from the south. This road, leading up from the Forth road bridge through Rosyth, is now a modern thoroughfare, carrying a constant two-way stream of traffic, but once it was only a track, a bridle-path, a pilgrim's way, a high road of history.

Through the centuries it has seen the passing up and down of ancient tribes — Picts, Scots and Caledonians — waging savage wars against the Roman invaders who occupied the country to the south for more than three hundred and fifty years. Then came raiding Vikings, Culdee priests, the storm-tossed company that escorted Edgar Atheling, his mother and sisters to Malcolm Canmore's Tower, and the armies of Edward the First of England. Perhaps William Wallace came stealing into the town at night to visit his mother. Robert the Bruce was seen both in defeat and in triumph, as were all the kings and queens who came to live in the Royal Palace and pray before the magnificent tomb of Margaret, Saint and Queen. Mary Stewart with a gay hunting party; the rabble of John Knox's followers who despoiled the great Abbey on their way to Stirling; James VI bringing his Danish bride to stay at the Palace; Prince Charles happily riding his pony and never dreaming of a cold January morning in Whitehall; Cromwell's troops hunting fugitives after the bloody battle of Inverkeithing; Jacobite patrols hastening up to the town to demand a levy from the city fathers, coaches plying between Dunfermline and Edinburgh by the ferry at North and South Queensferry, high bicycles jolting hard-wheeled over unmetalled surfaces, smoking cars that broke down on the hills; and on a fine summer day in 1889 Andrew Carnegie returning in coach-and-four, his mother by his side, to endow the place of his birth with the first Public Library.

There are, of course, other approaches to the town. From the west by Stirling, Alloa and Clackmannan or along the foot of the Ochils by Dollar and Saline; from the north over the moors that stretch down from Glendevon and Rumblingbridge; from the east through Kirkcaldy and Auchtertool or by Burntisland and Aberdour with its magnificent views of the Forth and the island of Inchcolm.

Dunfermline is surrounded on three sides by coalfields which used to yield a rich harvest, especially in the eighteenth and nineteenth centuries, with colleries that were famous in their day — Halbeath, Elgin, Wellwood from which came the famous Dunfermline Splint, with smaller seams to be found in North Urquhart and Pittencrieff where the monks mined coal in the eleventh century. A wide spreading network of motorways has considerably altered the appearance of the country round the town; farms have been swept away, unsightly housing-schemes have spread like a fungus over the rolling woods and small modern factories occupy sites by the motorway

The derivation of the name Dunfermline has been the source of some argument in the past and over the centuries the name has been found in many spellings, but it now seems to be more or less agreed that the word is a compound one of Celtic origin, dun signifying a fortified place and ferme meaning bent or crooked, referring to the sharp bend taken by the burn round the foot of Malcolm's Tower and lynne, a cascade or pool which is to be found at the waterfall there. The Tower burn rises in the north and follows a winding course through the town, down a narrow defile between wooded banks before it enters the beautiful policies of Pittencrieff Park, an estate gifted to the town by Andrew Carnegie. This park, now full of lawns and flowers,

Carnegie's statue in Pittencrieff Park looking up High Street to Townhouse, Dunfermline

was once a thickly-wooded wilderness, the haunt of wolves and bears and footpads who lay in wait to rob the unfortunate travellers of their belongings and sometimes their lives.

Other burns that played an important part in the town's economy, turning mills, filling lades, providing water for every purpose, were the Baldridge burn in the north-west, running at one time through the Elgin colliery and joining the Tower burn at what was once the Harriebrae spinning-mill, and the Lyne burn, which, rising in the moss to the north-east of Crossgates, ran by Halbeath, Woodmill, Brucefield and westwards along the south side of the town, where it met the Tower burn and, when joined by this tributary, greatly increased in size. It then turned south to enter the Forth at Charlestown. There were times when, swollen by heavy rains or melting snow, this burn flooded the rich, low-lying fields of Pittencrieff, Logie, Keavil and Pitliver, and the proprietors of these estates joined together to have a canal cut along a considerable length of the stream.

It was in the midst of the thick woods, watered by the Tower burn, high on a rocky mound outside the town, that Malcolm Canmore built his stronghold and with the coming of the king and his entourage, Dunfermline's personal history may be said to have begun. The exact date of its building is uncertain but might probably be about 1065. The town itself was a huddled collection of turf and wattle huts, surrounded by a protective mud wall with gates that could be closed and guarded when danger threatened. A Culdee settlement had been established but may by this time have exerted no influence if its originally strict discipline had become lax and corrupt and the priests offered little hope or help to the townsfolk in their desperate struggle against poverty, disease and starvation. So the decision of the king to build a tower near their village must have meant a great deal to them — work on the felling of trees the moving of rocks; the building of walls, that were six feet thick, making of steps up to the main door; a small drawbridge over a dry moat, a structure possibly of three storeys that contained about twenty large and small rooms. Other workmen were brought into the town — masons, carpenters, craftsmen of all kinds — and that meant more money to be made since these strangers had to be fed and housed. Royal patronage brought sudden prosperity to the struggling township.

Malcolm Canmore was a boy of nine when his father, King Duncan, was killed by Macbeth and he was sent for safe-keeping to the court of Edward the Confessor where he stayed till, at the age of twenty-three, destiny summoned him back to his native land to avenge his father's death and be installed at Scone as Malcolm the Third. Malcolm has often been represented as a rude, untutored savage, with a brutal nature, owing all his later success to the help given by his second wife, but this seems to be far from the truth. He was indeed a man of more than average intelligence, educated at the English court and able to speak four languages, including Norman French. His nickname of Canmore, which in the Gaelic means 'big head', referred to the fact that he was indeed his people's leader. His first wife was Ingibiorg, daughter of Earl Thorfinn and she brought him the powerful alliance of all the Scandinavians in the Orkneys and the north of Scotland. Of her, little is known, but she did bear him three sons before she died.

A few years later the whole country was shaken by the news of the Norman Conquest, an event which was to have an important effect on Malcolm and his kingdom. Edgar Atheling, heir to the English throne had been forced to flee before the Conqueror and with him he took his mother and his sisters, Margaret and Christine. There is a legend to the effect that contrary winds, perhaps miraculous in origin, drove their ship into the Forth but the argument put forward by Mr Freeman in his book *The Norman Conquest* seems a little more likely. In the autumn of 1069 Malcolm was in Durham, harrying the countryside in support of Edgar who, somewhere near York, was making his last forlorn stand against the forces of the Conqueror. In this he was completely defeated; he and his mother and sisters took ship and sailed for Monks Wearmouth where Malcolm had arrived with his army. Malcolm and Edgar had a conference and no doubt it was than that Malcolm invited the hapless family to take advantage of his hospitality at Dunfermline where he could offer them shelter while they discussed their next move. Malcolm stayed with his army and later returned to Scotland while the refugees, after an uneventful voyage, found their way safely to the Firth of Forth where they landed in a little bay, still known as St. Margaret's Hope. Messengers from Malcolm brought members of his household hastening to meet the travellers and to make them welcome in the Tower above the burn.

Princess Margaret had been born in Hungary about 1045; her father Edward had been forced to flee from King Canute and had, with his family, remained abroad for several years so that, when he was summoned back to

England as Atheling or heir to Edward the Confessor, he was regarded as a foreigner. After his death his son Edgar became heir apparent, but when Edgar the Confessor died, Harold and not Edgar was hailed as king. After the battle of Hastings and Harold's death Edgar was recalled but before he could be crowned William the Conqueror had seized the throne.

It is possible that Margaret and Malcolm might have met at the old king's court on her family's return from exile when she was about nine and he some fourteen years older. She was now a beautiful and intelligent young woman of twenty-four and the marriage which Malcolm presently proposed might not have been merely a politic matter with an eye to the future and the English Royal family's return to the throne. Margaret herself was inclined to refuse. In an age when royal princesses were provided with husbands while still children, she had remained unmarried; for, being a very devout Catholic, she had been hoping to enter a convent on her return to the Continent. But perhaps the urgings of her family, together with a feeling of duty and some affection for the powerful, red-bearded, quick-tempered and lusty man who was Scotland's king persuaded her to accept his proposal.

So, 'Queen Margaret was married to King Malcolm the Third with great solemnity at his village and castle of Dunfermline-in-the-woods, a place so strongly fortified that scarce man nor beast might tread its trackless paths.'

The marriage proved to be a fortunate one for Malcolm and for Scotland. Margaret was accustomed to life at the English court and she lost no time in introducing some splendour into Malcolm's state, increasing the number of his attendants and seeing that he was served on gold and silver plate. She disapproved of the casual manner in which Malcolm's retinue left the table after meals, so she introduced the saying of 'grace'. To persuade the knights to remain for the little ceremony she sent a cup of wine round the table afterwards. This was known as 'the grace-cup' and later became the loving-cup which, for centuries, was passed round Scottish tables.

Margaret had been brought up by the Benedictines or

Black monks and soon she was urging her husband to enlarge the little church of the Culdees with a finer edifice for Benedictines. It was to be known as the Church of the Holy Trinity and to serve as a place of Royal burial in the years to come. As time passed Margaret made many gifts to the Church, including jewels of great value, vessels of gold and silver curiously wrought and also a Black Cross 'full of diamonds' which she had brought out of England. According to Turgot the Queen's confessor and biographer, she performed many devout acts. 'Every morning she prepared food for nine little children, all indigent orphans. On her bended knees she fed them. With her own hand she ministered at table to crowds of poor persons and washed the feet of six children every evening. After the service she fed twenty-four persons and then, and not till then, she retired to a scanty, ascetic meal'.

In addition to all this the Queen found time to give birth to six sons and two daughters during the twenty odd years of her married life, so that the Tower above the glen must

Malcolm Canmore's Tower

have been filled to overflowing before some of them departed to set up establishments of their own.

In the end Malcolm and Margaret met with tragedy. He was killed along with his eldest son Edward at the battle of Alnwick. She was lying ill in the Castle of Edinburgh and when they brought her the news she did not survive the shock. Later, fearing that their uncle Donal Bain, rival claimant to the throne, might desecrate their mother's body, her younger sons took the corpse in secret from the Castle. The thick mist that descended to shield their passage through the ranks of Donal Bain's besieging army was then regarded as the first miracle connected with Queen Margaret's name. Her remains were taken across the Forth by the ferry and laid before the High Altar 'with great reverence and honour' in what was to prove a temporary resting-place.

In the years that followed Margaret's death, during the reigns of her three sons, Edgar, Alexander the First and David the First, the Church of the Holy Trinity received many Royal gifts. The Culdee Church and its influence had been completely supplanted by the religious ideas of the Roman church which with the approval of Margaret and Malcolm had been spreading through the whole country. About this time Alexander is supposed to have created Dunfermline into a Royal Burgh; he also bequeathed to the Church the Chapel of Stirling Castle together with a mansion in Edinburgh and some civic privileges by which the church authorities could hold their own courts and give judgment either by combat, fire or water. Alexander was responsible for bringing back his father's remains from England to be interred in the Royal sepulchre and he did much to enlarge and beautify the Church.

But when David the First came to the throne he decided that something more magnificent must be attempted. In the beginning David's reign had been a turbulent one, as he had to deal with various uprisings in the country as well as supporting the English King Henry's daughter against the usurper Stephen. But in peaceful times he was able to turn his attention to the founding of monasteries and other religious institutions. His Queen, Matilda, widow of the

Earl of Northampton died seven years after he came to the throne and as the chronicler says 'he took such grief at her death that he could not give his mind to marry another and passed the residue of his life without company of all women'.

Owing to his long connection with England and its culture, David had some knowledge of Anglo-Norman architecture and when he decided to build a Benedictine Abbey at Dunfermline he imported skilled masons and

Dunfermline Abbey from Pittencrieff Park

stone dressers who, when their work at Dunfermline was done, left their personal 'marks' on the walls and probably moved on to build Norman churches like those at Leuchars and Dalmeny. The people of the neighbourhood round Dunfermline must have viewed this great enterprise with awe and interest, for the building of it would assure them of work for years to come — clearing the site, quarrying building stones and limestone, cutting and carting timber to be hewn and carved by fine craftsmen.

Strangers, wearing foreign clothes and speaking in foreign tongues, arrived in the town with their apprentices and needed lodgings and this meant more money for the housewives who had a corner to spare.

At this time the town itself seemed to be divided in two by the Tower burn, the greater part of the houses being on the east side by the growing walls of the Abbey, while a few buildings crowned the raised land overlooking the glen from what is now Bridge Street. These had been in the protection of Malcolm Canmore's Tower, which remained the property of the King even after the policies of Pittencrieff had been given to the de Obervilles. In 1291 William de Oberville granted to the monks of Dunfermline the right to work coal for their own use in the lands of Pittencrieff on the condition that no arable land was disturbed.

It might be added here that the de Obervilles did not long enjoy their possession of Pittencrieff estate. They sided with the wrong claimant to the throne during the Wars of Independence and when Robert the Bruce was victorious he gave the forfeited lands to one of the Wemyss family who had been among his loyal supporters. This family was to hold Pittencrieff till about 1600. In 1538 the lands of Pittencrieff, Gallowrig and Clune were erected into a barony as a reward for good service to the King at home and abroad, and every time a successor came into his inheritance the Register of Sasines confirmed that the boundary between barony and burgh was the burn as far north as Wooers' Alley.

Malcolm Canmore's Tower, deserted by the court to live in Edinburgh Castle or the Abbey guest-house, which was later known as the Palace, still belonged to the King and the site did not become part of Pittencrieff estate till 1750 when Colonel Arthur Forbes of Pittencrieff acquired it in exchange for another piece of land near the Heugh Mills. As there are said to be signs of a later building on the Tower site it may have housed the official known as the King's Praepositus who collected the King's rents and was responsible for looking after the royal domain. There was also the Sheriff who held his courts in the open and Tower Hill may well have been the place chosen, while the Sheriff court of Fife continued to meet on the moot hill at Cupar till the sixteenth century.

The Parochial Church, comprising the Nave, was dedicated in 1150 and three years later, King David, having been smitten with a grievous illness, was found dead, kneeling before his mother's sacred Black Rood, and was buried in his own Abbey. He had reigned for twenty-nine years and had brought to Scotland a certain measure of peace, but his own life had been beset with tragedy for of the two sons and two daughters borne to him by his beloved wife Matilda none lived long enough to survive him.

During the reigns of the Kings that followed David — his grandson Malcolm IV, the Maiden and William the Lion — both the Abbey and the town of Dunfermline grew in importance. The list of Abbey officials was long. It began with the Abbot, Prior, sub-Prior. The office of Bailie or Steward was usually held by a distinguished layman of the locality; then there was the Sacristan, who was in charge of the vessels and ornaments of the altar and church, as well as the robes, candles, chalices; the Precentor or Chanter who led the choir-service, taught the boys music and was keeper of the Abbey seals, missals, and breviaries; the Librarian, who occupied an apartment near where the Abbey records books and manuscripts were kept in what was called the Scriptorium or Writing-room where the monks worked for set hours daily, transcribing holy books.

The Thesaurer or Treasurer collected the revenues and settled all the Abbey accounts and wages, while the Chamberlain who was in charge of the Wardrobes and dormitories, provided what was required by the Abbot or Prior when they set out on a journey. The Cellarer superintended the Abbey store house and supplied food and wine for the Monastery tables, the Refectioner took care of the plates, dishes and cooking utensils and ordered the arrangement of the food upon the table in the Refectory. The Almoner distributed meals, clothing and money to the poor who assembled at the monastery gates. He also visited them in their own homes and supplied their most immediate needs. The Hospitaller superintended the Hospice or Guest chamber and provided accommodation for strangers and itinerant beggars. Strangers of rank were entertained by the Abbot. The Infirmarian had charge of the sick of the monastery and administered the medicines prescribed by the Physician and, on urgent occasions, acted as Confessor to the dying. The Master of the novices looked after the training of young boys who were on trial in the Abbey for admission to the Order, the stables were in the charge of a Stable master and the Magister Operis or Master of Works, kept the buildings in repair. The Porter lived beside the gates and had the power to admit or refuse people wishing to enter. There was also a chief cook, a brewer, a carpenter, a forrester-huntsman with their numerous trains of subordinates who were generally laymen living outside the Monastery walls. These included the Abbey masons, wrights, tailors, plasterers, shepherds and farmers.

The building of the Abbey was completed by a great Cross Church, with transepts, choir, lantern-tower, presbytery lady chapel and chapter house so that the modest church founded by Malcolm and Margaret about a hundred and fifty years earlier was turned into something most magnificent. The cloisters were constructed along the south outside wall of the Church, along the front of the chapter-house on the east, along the outside of the north wall of the Monastery and the east wall of the dormitory, thus forming a covered walk of about 420 feet in circuit. The number of monks was increased from thirty to fifty and in 1243 Dunfermline became a mitred Abbey, Pope Innocent IV conferring on the Abbot of Dunfermline the honour and privilege of using the mitre, the ring, the crozier and the shoes. Pope Innocent also acceded to a request from the Abbot and Convent that 'considering the frigid region where the Abbey was situated the monks might be allowed to wear caps or bonnets'.

So the scene was set for what was to prove one of the most important events in the history of the town, the event that was to make the name of Dunfermline recognised and revered in the farthest corners of the civilised world.

Andrew Carnegie's birthplace — circa 1900

2
Robert the Bruce

On the 13th of July 1250 the young King Alexander III, his mother, various bishops, prelates and members of the nobility came to Dunfermline Abbey to assist in the translation of the remains of Malcolm Canmore's Queen Margaret, who had recently been canonised by Pope Innocent IV. This had been largely brought about by the efforts of Robert the Lord Abbot, recently made Lord High Chancellor of Scotland and evidently a man of some energy and ambition. The miracles attributed to Margaret, consisting of brilliant light flashes coming from her tomb, had been verified by the Bishop of St. Andrews and, the Pope having accepted this testimony, a splendid new tomb and shrine had, during the last eight months, been prepared for the reception of her remains. After lying in a stone tomb for over a hundred and fifty years, these remains could be expected to consist of a skull and some bones but when the tomb was opened such an agreeable perfume arose that the whole sanctuary was thought to be full of flowers.

According to Fordoun, when the saint's coffin was being carried towards the Choir and had reached the place where her husband's remains were lying in a tomb in the nave of the outer church 'the arms of the bearers were immediately benumbed and they could not convey the shrine with its relics further, on account of the greatness of the weight. After some interval additional and stronger bearers of the shrine being got, the more they endeavoured to raise it, the less able were they to do so. At length, all wondering, a bystander, divinely inspired, was heard suggesting distinctly that the bones of the Holy Queen could not be transferred till the tomb of her husband was opened and his body raised with similar honour. This saying pleased all and, adopting his advice, King Alexander, his lineal descendant with associates chosen for this purpose, without any either force or impediment, raised aloft the shrine filled with the bones of the King, along with the elevation of the coffer with the relics of the Queen, deposited in due form in a sarcophagus in the mausoleum prepared for that purpose, accompanied by the chanting convent and choir of prelates'.

It is a romantic story and only the cynical would dwell on the fact that Malcolm's tomb stood in the way of the daily processions, making a break in the fine view of the interior of the new choir and that this peculiar occurrence solved more than one of the Lord Abbot's problems.

This Robert de Kildeleth, Lord Abbot of Dunfermline, seems to have been a remarkable man. 'Learned in theology, acute in the art of law, sagacious and of polite address, he was full of energy and adroitness'. During his term of office which lasted ten years, he was frequently in communication with the Pope Innocent IV and in the Register of Dunfermline there are twenty-one of the Pope's Bulls, regarding the rights, privileges and grants concerned with the Abbey. When Robert became Abbot in 1241 the finances were at a low ebb owing to the cost of the recent extensive building programme and it may well be that the canonisation of Queen Margaret may have occurred to him as a perfect solution to the problem. In this he succeeded, although in those days the Court of Rome was very cautious in granting such honours; after five years of negotiations he had the satisfaction of seeing his efforts crowned with success. It is unfortunate that in the end Robert's ambitious career ended in disaster. Apparently he became implicated in the plot to have the bastard daughter of Alexander II legitimised so that she would be able to succeed the boy-king Alexander III in the event of his death. For this he was forced to resign all his high offices as Abbot of Dunfermline and Chancellor of Scotland; he went into retreat as a monk of Newbattle Abbey and was Abbot of Melrose when he died in 1273.

As a footnote to the story of St. Margaret's translation it is interesting to learn that, in consequence of this trouble about Malcolm's final resting place, he was also canonised and enrolled in the Catalogue of the Saints with his saint's day on June the second.

St. Margaret's Shrine lay on the upper plinth of the tomb, under a highly-ornamented stone canopy, supported by slender stone pillars. This Shrine consisted of a carved oaken cabinet, containing a magnificent silver chest, lavishly adorned with gold and precious stones. The relics it contained consisted of some bones and her skull with a long tress of auburn hair still flowing from it. Candles in tall silver sconces were kept burning night and day round the shrine.

Saint Margaret's Day was on the tenth of June, though, in later centuries the date was occasionally altered. Her effigy also appears on the burgh seal of 1589 and on the obverse of the coquet seal of the Regality of Dunfermline, which had a brass matrix and was granted to the town by Robert the Bruce in 1322. St. Margaret's Black Cross or Rood, given by her to the Church of Dunfermline was held in great veneration and pilgrims also visited her oratory which was a cave in the side of the glen by the burn. Other places connected with her name were St. Margaret's Well, now Headwell, St. Margaret's Hope, a sheltered bay on the Forth where she landed when she first came to Scotland, and St. Margaret's stone between Rosyth and Dunfermline on which she was supposed to have rested on her frequent journeys through the countryside. This large slab of freestone has been moved more than once but it can still be seen, set back from the carriage way not far from the gates of Pitreavie Castle.

From this time onwards till the War of Independence, Dunfermline's history is closely bound up with that of the Abbey, bulls and charters granted, resignation of lands into the hands of the Abbot, an increasing number of monks and laymen employed about the outside work of the Monastery. The town itself was also prospering. It enjoyed the privileges of a Royal Burgh, electing twelve burgesses who had to see that the various tradesmen went honestly about their work, though there seems to have been some distinction made as to the relative importance of such trades. No magistrate was permitted to brew ale or bake bread except for his own household needs; before butchers, dyers and shoemakers could become burgesses they had to change their occupation. Every burgh had its annual fair which combined business with pleasure and even in times of peace every man in the town had to take his turn in keeping watch from curfew till dawn. Cloth seems to have been the most important article of trade but from the list of commodities that had to pay toll the citizens of Dunferm-line apparently enjoyed some unexpected luxuries. Almonds, raisins, figs, rice, pepper, ginger and alum — the Scottish standard of living must have been more than equal to that of England or the Continent. Couriers to the Lord Abbot kept them all informed of the doings in the outside world and various Royal interments involved the interest and concern of the whole town.

In 1274 Margaret, wife of Alexander III and daughter of Henry III of England died at Cupar Castle and was interred in the Choir of the Abbey near King David's tomb; six years later all Scotland was mourning the deaths of her two sons, Prince David and Prince Alexander, aged only eighteen and twenty respectively. They died within a few months of each other. They were the heirs apparent to the throne and their deaths left only Alexander's daughter Margaret who was married to the King of Norway. It seemed that the Scottish knights would not welcome a woman wearing the Crown, regarding it as 'disgraceful for them to obey the words of such a one'. So Alexander, being pressed by his Lords of Council to find another wife, accepted the rather hasty choice of his ambassadors and married at Jedburgh, Yolande, the beautiful daughter of the Comte de Dreux. There was considerable gossip about this marriage as rumour reported that Yolande had been destined for a convent and had been 'stolen from God as a bride for Alexander' and so no-one was greatly surprised when, five months later, riding through a wild and stormy night, Alexander was killed as a result of a fall from his horse near Burntisland.

By this time Margaret, Queen of Norway, was dead, leaving behind her only daughter and it was this three-year old child, also called Margaret, who now became the infant Queen of Scotland.

This was, of course, the source and cause of all the troubles that befell Scotland in the years to come, but the story of Dunfermline was not greatly affected till Edward the First, King of England, paid his first visit to the town in 1291. After the death of Margaret's little daughter, there had been several claimants to the empty throne, each with their ardent band of supporters, and Edward, seeing himself as some Overlord of the country, had come to Scotland to exert his authority. Earlier at Norham and in a field on the north bank of the Tweed, eight of the claimants, including John Balliol, acknowledged the English King as Lord Paramount of Scotland and by the eleventh of June every castle was placed in his hands, to be held by him till two months after he had made his choice among the candidates. He was making his way in a royal cavalcade to Perth when he and his train of English nobles rode up the hill to Dunfermline and passed below the towering walls of the Monastery to visit the Abbey where, some in the chapter house and some before the high altar, imperiously summoned, various persons of all ranks — earls, barons, bishops, abbots, burgesses, sheriffs and the like — came to sign his roll of homage as his vassals. The names of William Wallace and Robert the Bruce were not among them though the latter did, at a later date, do homage to Edward for his English estates.

King Edward made other visits to the town, in 1296 and in 1303 when he spent most of the winter enjoying the hospitality of the Lord Abbot. This he repaid when he departed for Cambuskenneth in February 1304, by leaving orders for the Monastery to be destroyed by fire. Such barbarous behaviour has been explained by the fact that what Edward considered to be an illegal Parliament had been held in the great hall of the Monastery but Henderson in his Annals tells a more romantic story.

It seems that Wallace, an outlaw because of his stubborn refusal to acknowledge the authority to the English King over Scottish affairs, had come to Dunfermline to visit his aged mother, hiding from his pursuers in the wilderness of the glen until he was forced to flee for refuge in the west. It was then that his mother was supposed to have died and been buried secretly in the north portion of the Abbey churchyard. Soon after this Edward and his court arrived to take up residence in the Monastery and he was so enraged at the part the Abbot and his monks had played during her last days that he found in this an additional reason to destroy the Monastery. This conflagration seems to have been confined to the monastic buildings south of the Church, destroying the noble Fraters' Hall, which stretched from near the great western window in the hall to the west gable of the Church, the infirmary, lavatory, kitchen, stables and charter house.

It is reported that Edward returned to the town some six months later but he only stayed a night for, though the monks were already re-building their shattered walls, there would have been no suitable place for him to lodge. This may have been the reason that the monks decided to build a guest-house which came to be known as the Palace. It was built of sandstone, faced with unpolished ashlar, and was strongly buttressed against the steep slope of the hill, rising upon one side of the ravine through which the Tower burn flowed. Inside the Palace were royal suites, reached by narrow, twisting stairs with views to the south through windows set deep in the massive walls. The wife and daughters of Robert the Bruce knew the place when it was newly-completed, hastily furnished for their occupation, and they were followed, down the centuries, by generations of kings and queens and royal children.

A pend was built that spanned the roadway and connected the Palace with the Monastery while stables and courtyards stretched out on either side of the steep highway which plunged into the wooded depths of the glen and led away towards the west. Both Abbey and Palace were outside the limits of the town and all traffic had to pass through the West Port or 'wee pend' which stood in the

Dunfermline Palace ruins with the Abbey in the background

middle of St. Catharine's Wynd. Beyond lay the Kirkgate, with the Maygate and, higher up, the Hiegate, branching off to the right up the hill. In this, the oldest part of the town, lived the most well-to-do citizens in houses built above their shops and stores. Already benefiting by the growing importance of the Abbey and Royal Patronage, these merchants were to benefit still further from various Royal Charters made on their behalf.

In 1322 King Robert the Bruce granted a coquet seal to the Regality Court of Dunfermline which meant that the Abbey was authorised to collect customs in the name of the King. The Lord Abbot also gave a Charter to the Burgesses and Community of Dunfermline which allowed them access to various pastures and woods in the neighbourhood where the citizens could graze their cattle. The annual payment from the community to the Lord Abbot was one pair of white Paris gloves or sixpence sterling on the feastday of the Blessed Queen Margaret in addition to the usual feu-duty.

The Chartulary or Register of the Abbey did not fall into Edward's hands but, owing to the disturbed state of the realm, there were only a few entries before Bruce's accession. In 1315 he granted by charter a free gift to the Abbey of the Vicarage of Inverkeithing, to defray the charges of maintaining in perpetuity a lighted wax candle before the shrine of Saint Margaret in the choir. In 1323 on the fifth of March his wife Queen Elizabeth, gave birth at Dunfermline to a son who was later to become David the Second. Elizabeth was the daughter of Aymer de Burgh, Earl of Ulster; she died at Cullen Castle in 1327 and she was interred shortly afterwards in the Choir of Dunfermline Abbey.

Robert himself had only two more years to live and he spent much of this time in Dunfermline for he found the waters of Scotland Well of benefit. The popular belief is that Robert the Bruce died of leprosy and historians have spent a great deal of their time and energy arguing about the matter. The rumour about this disease seems to have been started by an entry in the Chronicon of Lanercost, at Carlisle, probably written by one of the gossip-loving, Robert-hating itinerant friars Minorities, who made Lanercost their headquarters. It is significant that the historians of the time — Fordoun, Wynton and Barbour, Archdeacon of Aberdeen — make no reference to leprosy and only mention the King's long sickness as the result of his arduous and exhausting campaigns, when he suffered great exposure and sustained various wounds. The likelier reason for the King's death was inflammation of the kidneys which gradually poisoned his system till he died at last of heart failure at the age of fifty-four.

This was on the seventh of June 1329 and his body was brought with 'great reverence and dignity' from Cardross to its last resting-place in the Abbey.

According to Barbour:
I hope that none that is on life
The lamentation can describe
That folk for their Lord made.
And when they long thus sorrowed had
They have him had to Dunfermline

And him solemnly erded syne
In a fair tombe into the Quire . . .
And syne upon another day
Sorry and wo they went their way —
And he debowelled was cleanly
And als balmed syne full richly,
And the worthy Lord of Dowglas
His hart, as it forespoken was,
Received has in great daintie
With great and fair solemnitie.

The good Sir James Douglas thus received the 'noble heart' which, on his way to the Holy Land, he was to carry only as far as Spain where he himself was killed, and Sir Gilbert Harding who had helped to guard Bruce at Bannockburn, made the funeral oration. In the Chamberlain's Rolls are some interesting details regarding the expenses incurred for the King's funeral — fine linen, great quantities of gold leaf, 32½ stones of wax for candles, fees to masons, apothecaries, horses for the litter, mantles of black bugets (lamb's skin fur) for the knights, meals for the paupers, wine for the preaching friars of Perth. The white marble monument later erected to the King's memory was made by Richard Barber in Paris, workmen carried it to Bruges where it was put on the Abbot's ship and transported probably to North Queensferry on the Forth. No description of this tomb remains but Fordoun has preserved Bruce's epitaph, translated from the Latin.

'Here lies the invincible Robert, blessed King. Let him who reads his exploits repeat how many wars he carried on. He led the Kingdom of Scots to Freedom by his uprightness; now let him live in the Citadel of Heaven'.

Regality House, Nether Town

3
Town ports

At this time Bruce's son, David, born in Dunfermline Palace, was only nine years old. At the age of five he had been married to Johanna, seven-year-old daughter of the English King Edward II, and after King Robert's death the two children were crowned at Scone with special ceremonial as the Pope had sent a Bull that for the first time permitted anointing. As David was too young to rule, Thomas, Earl of Moray, was made Regent. He had been the late King's brother-in-law and one of the leaders at the battle of Bannockburn, and when Edward Balliol seized the chance to lay claim to what he considered to be his father's crown, Moray had to raise an army to defend the boy-king. Unfortunately he met with death — by poison, it was said — while at Musselburgh and once again Dunfermline Abbey resounded to the requiem for a great man, as the Regent was laid to rest below the Lady-chapel.

Scotland naturally felt the loss of these two powerful leaders and the years that followed were uneasy ones, full of wars. Battles like Dupplin and Halidon Hill were fought; Welsh mercenaries hired by Balliol, Edward with English forces, ravaged the countryside, while the two Royal children were sent to France for safety. They stayed there for seven years and when they came back to Scotland in 1341, landing at Inverbervie in Kincardineshire, they were given a warm welcome. But David knew little of his country or his people and in the end, when war broke out again with England, he was made prisoner at the battle of Neville's Cross and taken south to London to be lodged in the Tower. He was kept a hostage in England for eleven years, his ransom being a heavy drain on Scotland's resources.

No doubt Dunfermline townsfolk suffered from famine and disease like the rest of the country, but the life of the town, centred round the Abbey, seemed to go on much as usual. One or two local details are of interest.

In the time of Robert the Bruce the possessions even of a rich merchant were scanty enough, as shown in a will of that period: 'Ane best-board or table with a board cloth, ane towel, ane basin, ane laver the principal bed with sheets, ane feather-bed, ane barrel, ane water-pot, ane posset, ane bag to hold money, ane cart or chariot, ane large brasspot and little pot and pan, ane roasting-iron, ane griddle, ane mortar and pestle, ane dish, ane dibbler, ane charger, ane cuppie.'

The town of Kirkcaldy, already mentioned as a burgh in 1304, was dependent, with its harbours, on the Abbey of Dunfermline. In 1355 a Parliament was held at Dunfermline to elect Sir Andrew Moray Regent. In 1341, when Ambassadors from France visited Scotland to persuade David II to invade England, Edinburgh could not find sufficient accommodation for the large and noble retinue, so some crossed the Forth to lodge in the Royal guest-house. In the winter of 1343 King David and his Queen Johanna stayed for a while at the Palace, where he sealed a number of Royal Charters. Later on, in 1363, he gave a confirmation charter to the Regality and authorised burgesses of Dunfermline, Kirkcaldy, Musselburgh and Queensferry to buy and sell wool, hides, skins and other merchandise freely and without impediment. He was careful, however, to reserve to himself the Great Customs from wool, hides and skins. His charter was witnessed by 'William, Bishop of St. Andrews, Patrick, Bishop of Brechin, our Chancellor, Robert, Steward of Scotland, our nephew William, Earl of Douglas, Robert de Erskyn, our Chamberlain, Archibald Douglas and John Huth, Knight. Given at Edinburgh the 24th day of September, in the thirty-fourth year of our reign.'

The establishment of a public Tron for Customs

administration would no doubt follow this charter, with the various ports of the town being manned to collect tolls and examine merchandise. The ports that came into being at this time were the West Port, in St. Catharine's Wynd, the Mill or Collier Row Port at the top of Bruce Street, the Rottenrow Port near the top of Chapel Street, the Crosswynd Port at the top of Crosswynd, East Port, at the east end of the Highgate, the Tolbooth Port at the foot of Bruce Street. Tolls were collected at these ports and taken to a clerk at the Booth, a small shop, for entering in his collecting book. This was the origin of the name Tolbooth and later, when the booth was connected with a prison, the prison gradually became known as the Tolbooth.

The Market cross was erected about this period, probably a tall stone pillar set on the top of a few steps.

In 1368 the Chapel and hospital of St. Leonard's was built in the 'villa inferior' or Nethertown, a site now occupied by St. Leonard's linen factory. The oldest records concerning this charitable institution date back only to 1594, but in 1651 an entry appears which connects the hospital with Malcolm and Margaret. The tradition that Queen Margaret was the foundress is possibly right. The object of the institution was to support eight widows who were each entitled every year to four bolls of malt, eight loads of coal each worth about fourpence, eight lippies of fine wheat, eight lippies of groats, fourteen loads of turf, with an apartment in the hospital. At one time two shillings a year were allowed for their personal expenditure. A graveyard adjoined the hospital and the last recorded interment took place in 1700. It is generally believed that the destruction of chapel and hospital was the work of Cromwell's soldiers when they entered the town after their victory at Inverkeithing in August 1651 but according to an entry at a meeting of the Provincial Synod of Fife, held in Dunfermline in April, 1651, three months before the battle, a supplication was presented for the re-building of the hospital. The chapel is not mentioned and it is unlikely to have been maintained after the Reformation a hundred years earlier. At one time houses apparently built from the stones of the hospital and chapel were to be seen in the neighbourhood but these have long since disappeared. It is not recorded what happened to the last eight widows and their fourteen loads of turf.

Hospitals in these days could be of various types. Some were founded as homes for the sick or to provide a bed and nourishment for pilgrims and travellers. Others sheltered the aged and infirm as well as orphan children, or gave protection to lunatics or supervised the segregation of lepers. Some were medical charities, some non-medical, while many comprised both. Generally speaking, hospitals were either connected with monasteries or derived from the pious offering of the laity, while the buildings themselves could be of all shapes and sizes. They all had in common a chapel and sometimes a burying-ground.

After the Reformation the revenues of some hospitals, almshouses and bedeshouses were appropriated by lairds who could then grant feu charters of the lands and rents, but others were maintained. In a humble supplication from the poor people of the realm to the King and Parliament in 1581 it seems that some lairds 'demolished goodly houses that were appointed for the receiving alms and having applied the same to their particular uses'. Some attempt by Acts of Parliament and a specially-appointed commission under the Earl of Argyle to remedy these abuses was made but apparently little was done. In the hospitals that survived the Reformation the restrictions placed upon their inmates were much more severe than in the earlier institutions. At the Edinburgh Leper Hospital, for instance, which was not established till 1591. The rules of the hospitals were enforced under pain of death and, that this might not be thought to be an empty threat, a gallows was erected at the gable end of the building for the summary execution of offenders.

Outside the town were two sanctuaries, one at the Girth Bow and the other in a refuge-house on the north side of the Maygate which was not removed till 1819. There was also the Grange, situated about a mile south of the Abbey, from which the monks obtained their grain and other produce. In 1374 some of the Dunfermline mills are mentioned in old documents for the first time. A small corn mill at the

Collier Row Port, sometimes called the Mill Port, at the
top of Bruce Street; the mill of Our Lady in Nethertown,
where the site still retains the name of Lady's Mill; the
Abbey Mill in Monastery Street.

But the tranquil, prospering life of the town may once
more have been rudely interrupted when Dunfermline
again received the doubtful attentions of an English King,
this time Richard II. Froissart says 'when the king and his
lords left Edinburgh, they went to Dunfermline, a tolerably
handsome town, where is a large and fair Abbey of black
monks, in which the kings of Scotland have been accustomed to be buried. The king was lodged in the Abbey; but,
after his departure the army seized it and burnt both it and
the town.' Other sources, however, suggest that the English
did not at this time proceed beyond the Firth of Forth.

If any damage was done the energy and industry of the
monks would soon repair it, and four years later Ambassadors from England and France came to Dunfermline to
meet Robert II and his nobles and to renew the truce that
had been concluded earlier among the three countries. At
this time the Palace was becoming more and more popular
as a royal residence but even its spacious accommodation
must have been strained to house all the royal family when
Robert II was King. He had two wives and fourteen sons,
six of whom were legitimate. There were also eight
legitimate daughters and 'divers others'.

His eldest son, John, Earl of Carrick, married Annabelle
Drummond, the beautiful daughter of Sir John Drummond
of Stobhall and Menteith. She was a woman of great piety
and good sense; she made John a charming wife and later
Scotland hailed her as a most virtuous Queen, when her
husband John was crowned Robert III at Scone in 1390.
Like St. Margaret she was very devout and went on many
pilgrimages through the country but she preferred to make
her home in Dunfermline Palace and it is probable that,
like her son who was to be James I of Scotland, her family
of three sons and four daughters were all born here. Her
husband also gave her a small house in Inverkeithing, for
she was very fond of swimming in the sparkling waters of
Inverkeithing Bay and it was there she died in 1401, before

the tragedy that befell her eldest son David at Falkland or the capture of her son James by the English five years later. Of her the chronicler says 'Many daughters have done virtuously but thou excellest them all.'

Annabelle was buried in the Abbey, the last of the royal interments with the exception of that of the infant son of James VI in 1602.

East Port House

4
Prosperous Burgh

In 1435 Aeneas Silvius, afterwards Pope Pius II, visited
Scotland and what he says of the country in general may
well have applied to Fife and Dunfermline at that time. In
his opinion Scotland was a cold country, generally bare of
trees and producing only a few varieties of grain, but
possessing a sulphurous stone which was dug up and used
for making fires. The towns were unwalled, the houses
usually built of limestone and roofed with turf with a cow's
hide hung over the only doorway. The common folk he
found to be poor and uneducated, living on meat and fish
with bread a delicacy. 'The men are small in stature but
bold, the women fair and comely and prone to the pleasures
of love.' How, one wonders did this holy man know that?

The wine was all imported, the horses were small
ambling nags on which neither reins nor curry-comb was
ever used. The oysters were larger than in England and
from Flanders Scotland imported wool, salt, fish and
pearls.

In the fifteenth century a man of the town, who began in
poverty as a pedlar and worked hard to acquire forty
pounds Scots, could then buy a horse and cart. With
business improving he was able to lease a shop with a
counter, chests and Flemish coffers and soon he became a
merchant, making voyages to other countries. With luck he
could marry a rich wife, dress himself in silks on Sunday
with green or grey cloth for weekdays while his spouse
flaunted about in scarlet. In 1438 the sumptuary laws of
James II banned the wearing of gowns in silks or scarlet

cloth, unless worn by municipal officials, while women were to be content with short kerchiefs and little hoods.

By this time Dunfermline was beginning to assume the form and stature of a prosperous town. The population was

East Port

about twelve hundred with another seventy in the Abbey precincts. The houses occupied a restricted space between the various Ports, crowded in upon the narrow lanes and closes with the Tolbooth and market cross the centre of all the town's activities. At that time the town council was elected annually by an assembly of all the burgesses and its duties seem to have been very comprehensive. The magistrates were bound to see that the traders acted according to their laws, not interfering with each other's rights and liberties. The Chamberlain had to make a strict examination of all the weights and measures and collect the fines levied on those who cheated their customers. There were numerous regulations that the shopkeepers had to observe. Bakers must show their bread in their windows, pastry-cooks had to give samples of their wares to the Chamberlain who pronounced on their quality. Fleshers must keep good beef, mutton or pork and show samples of everything in their windows. Burgesses could claim the assistance of a flesher in killing off some of the stock of pigs or sheep or cattle for which food could not be found during the winter months. Fish was also examined and ale tasted for its quality and strength. No magistrate, while he was in office, could be a brewer.

The title of Alderman as applied to the Chief Magistrate of the town is to be found for seemingly the first time in 1395 in a charter from John, Abbot of Dunfermline and the Conventual Brethren to the Alderman and Community of Dunfermline. In this Charter or Indenture the town received important privileges in the way of customs, stallage, profits, fines and annual payment of rent and this may also mark the first use of the Burgh Seal which seems to have depicted in a rude fashion a gable of King Malcolm's Tower.

A BIT OF OLD DUNFERMLINE, NETHERTOWN.

Nethertown

The citizens were also expected to take part in the practice of archery and for this purpose Bow Butts were set up in the Nethertown. Later in the century about 1457 — an Act of Parliament enjoined every craftsman 'to cry down football and golf and to appear in the Parish Kirk and the butts thereof and to shoot six arrows thereat.' Even at that time there seems to have been considerable trouble about the game of football for it was prohibited in 1424 when James I had a statute directing that 'no man play at fitball under the penaltie of fifty shillings' and another saying that 'all men shall busk themselves to be archers from they be twelve years of age.' Later the King instituted military musterings or wappinshaws where the universal practice of archery was ordained while football and golf were 'utterly cried down.'

In these days every craftsman when wanted had to appear fully equipped with the weapons of war, clad sufficiently in armour with a hagbutt, while every man having ten pounds worth of land was expected to provide himself with 'ane basnet and ane glove of plate, with ane spear and sword. Wha has not ane basnet shall have ane gude havergeon and ane gude airn jack of his body and ane airn knapiskay an glove of plate. Every man having the value of a cow in goods shall have ane bow with ane schaff of arrows or ane spear.'

In spite of these warlike preparations, however, there had been, about twenty years earlier, a significant change in Dunfermline's importance as a rising Scottish town. After the murder of James I at Perth in 1436, it was decided that Perth, Stirling, Scone and Dunfermline were none of them capable of protecting Royalty against 'the designs of the nobility' and this was the reason why Edinburgh with its impregnable Castle was chosen as the future place of residence and refuge for the Royal family.

This decision did not, of course, affect the power of the Abbey and some years later James II gave it a Conformation Charter which contains some interesting items. The King confirmed all the gifts of his Royal predecessors from Malcolm and Margaret onwards, including Duncan, Edgar, Ethelrede, Alexander, Queen Sybilla, David I, William and Robert the Bruce. These gifts range from the shire of Kirkcaldy to mansions in Berwick, Roxburgh, Haddington, Edinburgh, Linlithgow and Stirling, from every seventh seal caught at Kinghorn to half the

blood of all the whales taken between the Forth and the
Tay. There was a free forest at Dollar, a toft with a croft in
the town of Clackmannan, the great customs of Dunfermline, Kirkcaldy, Musselburgh and the Queen's ferry,
besides five marks sterling from the revenue of the burgh of
Inverkeithing. No detail seems to have been omitted and
the massive list was signed by the King at Edinburgh on
the 22nd day of the month of March 1450 in the fifteenth
year of his reign. It was witnessed by a large number of
eminent men — William, Bishop of Glasgow, Chancellor
Lord Crichton, Andrew, Abbot of Melrose, Lord Somervil-
le, Lord Glamis, the Archdeacon of Glasgow and George of
Schoriswode, Rector of Culter. Who could have foretold
that in little more than a hundred years the great and
powerful Abbey with all its rich possessions would have lost
everything?

But as the century progressed there were to be found
increasing signs that the Roman Catholic Church as a
religious institution was falling into disrepute. Parish
priests had grown indolent and worldly, too lazy to preach
sermons and spending much of their time in ale-houses.
Itinerant friars seemed to share in the general corruption,
the sale of benefices had reached scandalous proportions
and even the great dignatories of the Church greedily
grasped at the wealthier revenues. In evidence of this there
can be quoted the case of the Double Election.

In 1472 the abbacy of Dunfermline having become
vacant, the monks chose one of their own number to be
Lord Abbot, but the King intervened, asking the Pope to
approve his own choice, Henry Crichton, Abbot of Paisley.
As Leslie in his History of Scotland says 'so then first began
sic manner of promotion of seculares to abbacies by the
King's supplication and the godly erectionis were frustrate
and decayit, because that the Court of Rome admitted the
Prince's supplications, the rather that they gat greit profeitt
and sowmes of money thairby; quarfoir the bishops durst
not confirme them that were chosen by the Covenant; nor
they quha were electit durst not pursew their own ryght,
being promoted furth of the court which livit courtlyke,
secularlye and voluptuouslye. And then seissit all religious

and godlye myndes and deidis, quhairwith the secularis and temporall men beand sklanderi with their evill example fell frae all devition and godlyness to thair warks of wickedness, quhairof they dailie makit evill did encrease.' It is evident that 'the outrage on the Convent of Dunfermline' created an unhappy precedent, for it was not long before further abuses were perpetrated. The superiority and revenues of religious houses were soon granted to bishops and secular priests who had not taken the monastic vows and were not qualified to preside in a monastery. This led to greater trouble when such charges were given to laymen or even children, all being done with the Papal authority on the excuse that such appointments were only temporary. It is clear now that this sort of thing could only lead to disaster and the crumbling of the Church before the fury of the Reformation.

In all of this the King himself was not guiltless. James IV displayed a great deal of religious zeal, eating no meat on Wednesdays and Fridays, hearing numerous masses and going on more than one annual pilgrimage but, like most Scottish kings, he was always short of revenue and he did not hesitate to make use of the wealth of the Church to benefit his relatives. When his brother, James, Duke of Ross, was only eighteen, the King secured for him the rich bishopric of St. Andrews and only a few months later he had him installed as Commendator of the wealthy Abbey of Holyrood. Not content with that, the King went on to make him Commendator of Dunfermline Abbey with Arbroath Abbey following two years later. The scandal this caused was not silenced by the death of the Commendator in 1504, for the King secured the archbishopric for Alexander, a boy of eleven, the eldest of his own illegitimate sons. This time it was felt in ecclesiastical circles that he had gone too far and the Convent of Dunfermline did not at once accept the King's nominee. It may have been to mollify the disgruntled monks that when the Pope, Julius II presented a sword of state and a consecrated hat to James IV it was delivered with some ceremony to the Abbey Church of Holyrood by the Papal Legate and the Abbot of Dunfermline, James Bethune, then on the threshold of a distinguished career. This sword of state is now in Edinburgh Castle and forms part of the crown regalia.

So far the annals of Dunfermline had not produced anyone of note but in the middle of the fifteenth century a man came to live in the town whose name was to linger down the centuries as that of a great poet. Little is known of Robert Henryson. He was probably born about 1425, received a liberal education and passed through the schools in the usual way, finally taking the degree of Master of Arts. On the tenth of September 1462 Master Robert Henryson Licentiate in Arts and Bachelor in Degrees was admitted a member of the newly-founded University of Glasgow. Later he settled in Dunfermline where he practised as a Notary Public. But there is reason to believe that he was also a schoolmaster in connection with the Abbey. His classical education is revealed in all his writings from the famous Testament of Cresseid to his witty versions of Aesop's Fables in the Scots metre which are full of lively descriptions and humorous comment, but his early Scots spelling and vocabulary make his work difficult to read today without a glossary. In his poem called 'Schir Chantelclar and the Fox, written about 1485 Henryson mentions the Orloge Bell which may refer to a striking clock in the Abbey precincts.

About this time — in 1488 — the town council records report the first meeting of the town council and Magistrates which set forth an interesting list of names — Provost David Couper, Bailies David Litster and William of Ballowne with fourteen Councillors, Spens, Malcolm, Alan, Brysson, Wallas, Stevyn, Clerk, Crawford, Thomson, Butler, Law, Gibson, Pierson and Hume. From this time on, the records are full of domestic matters from which much can be gleaned about the town and its citizens. In 1490, for instance, mention is made of a sklat house, probably the first in the town to be roofed with slate, and in 1491 there comes the earliest references to the weavers who were to make this trade the main industry of the town. Reference is also made at this time to the stocks, set up near the Pillory at the Tolbooth. No doubt these ominous objects became familiar enough to the townspeople down the years till they were removed, probably about the eighteenth century.

At the end of the fifteenth century there was only one street paved with causeway stones — the Casigate, afterwards the Hie Gate. All the other thoroughfares were called wynds, vennels, gaits or rows — such as the Collier Row, now Bruce Street, the Rotten Row, now Queen Anne Street, the Crosswynd, the Common Vennel, the Kirkgait, St. Catherine's Gait, Maygait, Newraw, Nethertoun, the Foul Vennel, now Canmore Street, then a muddy footpath running from the east end of the Maygait below the walls of the Abbey to the Newraw. Beyond the East Port there was a highway called the Gallowgait which led by Haly-Bluid Acres to the gallows tree and later on to the Witches' Dub.

Middens were piled high in front of the houses and every day the burgh head drove the burgesses' cattle through the town to the common pasture. This grazing of sometimes his only cow was just one of the citizen's privileges — he could collect turf and firewood on the wasteland and cultivate the ridges which were, by lot, assigned to him in the arable land, though some of the burghs were already beginning to feu or sell parts of their commons. As these usually consisted of undrained and over-cultivated land the crops were uncertain and scanty.

Although there were ports to the town there were no recognised town-walls, the backs and the yards of the houses forming the only protection against attack. These houses were being built closer and closer together and the number of trades followed by the citizens were also increasing in number and variety. Now there were smiths, masons, weavers, tailors, wrights, bakers, fleshers, shoemakers, brewers, dyers, waulkers and fullers of cloth, and cadgers who brought loads of fish to the town and Abbey on Wednesdays, Fridays and Saturdays. The town was prospering and, despite the whispered gossip about what went on in the Abbey and its monastery, Provost Couper with his Councillors, must have faced the future with some confidence.

After all the alarms and excursions that had troubled

Scotland during the reign of James III, culminating in his mysterious murder in the Mill of Bannockburn, the coronation of his son James IV at Scone seemed to promise some improvements, though the country was still wracked with civil strife and the King, a boy of fifteen, would always be haunted by the guilt he felt for his father's death. James had been a sickly infant and when another son had been born he also had been christened James so that the line could follow on with the name that had been borne by every Scottish King for the last hundred years. But James thrived and soon after his Coronation he came to Dunfermline, crossing the Forth at the ferry, and later the Palace became one of his favourite residences. All his life James was interested in the castles and palaces that belonged to him. A new palace at Holyrood, towers and a barbican at Stirling Castle, the south side of Linlithgow Palace, a charming new hunting lodge at Falkland, set beside the haunted old castle, with various other towers and houses built throughout the more remote parts of his kingdom — all were constructed under his direction and no doubt he was responsible also for the various improvements in the great building at Dunfermline.

As he grew older the King became more restless and he spent most of his time moving from one royal residence to another, Edinburgh, Linlithgow, Stirling, and sometimes to Dunfermline which was always kept ready for the royal visitor, with such permanent furnishings as huge oak tables, straw matting or rushes on the floors and gaping fireplaces filled by enormous iron grates. The rest of the furnishings — richly-wrought gold and silver plate, tapestries to temper the draughts round the thick stone walls, beds with ornamented frameworks and hangings of rich damascened silk and velvet with the mattresses only a few inches from the floor — all were brought in the King's train which sometimes consisted of close on a hundred male and female servants, grooms, ushers, clerks, cup-bearers, turnspits, cooks, keepers of the candles, the napery and the coals, a barber, a tailor, a cutler, one to buy fish and dress capons and game. Some of these, of course, were of noble descent — in 1499 the Master of Gray was his cup-bearer and Sir Adrian Hepburn Master of the Stables, all with modest wages of some twenty marks a year. Provisions had already been brought to the Palace by the King's tenants who paid their rent in kind and the accumulation of these stores sometimes decided which castle or palace should be selected for his next residence. All his company was provided with free food and lodging and many of his attendants brought their own train of servants with them.

It is easy to imagine the stir and bustle that this invasion would bring to Dunfermline, filling the narrow wynds with the noise and glitter of men-at-arms, the sound of hunting-horns echoing among the thick woods of the glen, the windows of the Palace shining out through the darkness while the King and his court danced to the music of harps and fiddles.

Some accounts of the time provide interesting information about the King's apparel. Doublets were worn very open at the breast so that shirts and their laundering were of great importance. Thirteen hanks of gold thread were delivered to David Lindsay's wife 'to sew the Kingis sarkis'. With this he wore short russet leather boots, a surtout of fine cloth or velvet, richly embroidered with gold, a low velvet bonnet hooped with a diamond or a ruby fastening a graceful feather, while massive chains of pure gold lay on his chest, suspending his sword and hunting-horn. Half-boots were sometimes exchanged for velvet shoes indoors and the velvet bonnet replaced by a brown beaver while his loose dressing-gowns for wearing in his private suite were of fine satins, richly lined perhaps with fur and embroidered in gold.

The King's toilet table displayed much silver, including a silver clam for holding his tooth-powder. When he went on his expedition to the Western Isles the King was provided with 'ane cote and ane pair of breeks for the sea' while his room on board was hung with French tapestry.

Even after his marriage to Margaret Tudor, daughter of Henry VII of England, James' restlessness still took him to and fro through the country, hunting, gambling, listening to petitions and making pilgrimages. One of these was his annual visit to the shrine of St Duthac in Tain. Winter was approaching and at Dunfermline he was joined by the Queen who came from Stirling with thirty-five carts in her train. Having taken leave of her James set out with 'a poet, three falconers, four Italian ministrels, a Moorish drummer and a horse laden with silver plate.' While he was away, pest broke out in the town and he sent orders for the Queen to remove to Lindores Abbey, but she chose to remain till his return.

No doubt the doings of the King gave Dunfermline citizens plenty to talk about. James was always interested in inventions, he caused various changes in the coinage, he conferred with Sir Andrew Wood of Largo about the building of the great ship St Michael — which 'wasted all the woods of Fife' — he backed up the claim of Perkin Warbeck to the English throne and finally went to war against the English on behalf of the French — a war that led to the battle of Flodden. It was an unpopular war and it must have been with heavy hearts that Provost Couper and his councillors stood on the steps of the Tolbooth and watched the local lads, conscripted for the army, march away with flags flying and drums beating.

Children playing at the corner of Priory Lane 1901

5
St Margaret's Relics

Dunfermline, like all the rest of Scotland, must have taken a long time to recover from the tragedy of Flodden, which had robbed the town of so many strong and lusty young men. Women must have had to till the fields and reap the harvest, work the looms and keep the mill-wheels turning. Only old men were left to practise archery and toil at the forge and the armourer's bench.

The Abbey, too, was involved in stormy times as it had become involved with politics and the growing threat of enemies throughout the kingdom. In 1526 the Abbot James Beaton, who was also Archbishop of St Andrews, was present at a battle fought at Avonbridge near Linlithgow between the Earls of Lennox and Angus over the possession of the young King and had to flee from the field. For a time he lurked in the hills, disguised as a shepherd before he decided it was safe to return. No doubt this was why Angus, after the battle, descended upon Dunfermline and allowed his soldiers to pillage the Abbey.

The young King James V was growing up. He had come to resent the fact that under Angus' rule he was more a prisoner than a monarch and finally, having made careful plans, he escaped from Falkland when out with a hunting party. He rode hard for Stirling Castle where a loyal captain of the guard was waiting to welcome him. He was seventeen now, an eligible Prince and when he emerged to take charge of the government of the country, various excellent matches were put before him — a Princess of Portugal, the widowed Queen of Hungary, the daughter of the deposed King of Denmark with Norway as her dowry, Mary of Bourbon, Mary of England, his cousin. But in the end James, after studying their portraits, chose the lovely Magdalene, daughter of the King of France. He went to see the young lady, the couple fell in love at first sight and, though his advisers were not in favour of the match as the young lady was supposed to be very delicate, James had his way. There was a splendid wedding at Notre Dame in Paris, with the King a handsome figure in blue velvet, furred with sables and pantaloon hose of white satin, while she was a lovely bride in white damask, her gown sewn with gold and pearls. They were attended by an array of Scots earls, lords, bishops and barons, all in their best attire.

No doubt Dunfermline was in a festive mood when the King brought his Queen back to Scotland, landing at Leith where she knelt down to kiss the Scottish soil 'for the love she bore its King.' Preparations were put in hand for her coronation but before that could take place came the news of her death 'of a vehement fever. The grief of all was lamentable to behold.'

James, being a King, was allowed little time for his personal sorrow and it was not long before his Ambassadors called upon the Duke of Guise-Lorraine to arrange a match with his daughter Marie. The King married her by proxy, Lord Melville, and sent a fleet to convey her safely to Scotland, for Henry VIII had fancied the young woman for himself and was highly indignant that he should be supplanted by his nephew.

So once again James rode through Fife to St Andrews, there to welcome his new bride, who landed at Balcomie where she had been entertained by Sir James Learmonth. The passage of the Royal train through Fife with halts at several places en route before proceeding to cross the Forth at the Queen's ferry has been recorded by various chroniclers and in the State papers may be found some details of the expenditure involved.

'Item — for carrying of bedding and coferis with lynning claithe and ane coffer of the Master Stabiller to the Queen; ane chair and burd to the Queen from Sanctandrois to

Couper and Falkland and fra Falkland to Ravensheugh
and Dunfermline the space of five days summa — 52
shillings. Item — for carrying the Dames of Honouris
beddis fra Dunfermline to Edinburgh — five shilling.'

It was probably about this time that some alterations to
the Palace were made. An upper storey was added with
projecting bay windows on the west wall and large mullion
windows brought more light into the stone-walled rooms.
When this had been done the King and his court were
frequently in residence with representatives of the local
landed families in attendance.

The fortunes of King James V seemed to be prospering.
His French wife was charmed with her new subjects and
everyone was charmed with her, especially as she soon gave
birth to two sons. But the ill-luck of the Stewarts still
dogged the Royal footsteps. In a short space of time both
little boys were dead and the country once more without an
heir. There was no love lost between Scotland and
England. Scottish ships were seized on the orders of the
English King and James' demands for retribution went
unheeded. War rolled nearer and when Henry VIII raised
the old bogey of English supremacy James was goaded into
action. Unwilling action for he found little support among
his nobles but armies marched to the Borders and the
disunited Scots suffered the crushing disgrace of the
skirmish — it was little more — of Solway Moss in 1542.
After that James went to pieces. He sought refuge in
Falkland Palace where he died soon after he had received
the news that a daughter had been born to the Queen at
Linlithgow.

The citizens of Dunfermline must have found it difficult
to understand what was happening as various factions
quarrelled over the succession and the possession of the
baby-girl who was at last taken away to safety in France.
Perhaps they were occupied with affairs nearer home for,
recently, it had become obvious that the brethren of the
great religious houses, with their refusal to move with the
times, had fallen from their former high place in public
regard. The people in town and country knew only too
much about the corruption and double-dealing that went

on in convent and monastery, chapel and church, so they
were ready to answer Knox's rallying call when he
preached a rousing sermon in Perth in May 1559.

From the fifteenth century instead of genuine Abbots
who had been monks control of the Abbey passed to
Commendators who had not been monks and could not be
genuine Abbots though they were sometimes so styled. The
title was sometimes purely honorary and after the Reformation laymen obtained the office.

Now the following warrant indicates what the Reformation leaders were doing all over Scotland, issued with the
signatures of the Protestant lords — Argyll, Stewart and
Ruthven — giving permission for their 'trusty friends to
take down the images and bring them forth to the
Kirkyaird and burn them openly. Also to cast doun the
altars and purge the kirk of all kinds of monuments of
idolatry. And this ze faill not to do, as ze will do us
singulare empleasure and so committis you to the protection of God. From Edinburgh 1560.'

In January of this year George Durie Abbot or Commendator of Dunfermline and the Earl of Eglinton had
prudently passed from Dunbar to France. Thus the line of
Dunfermline Abbots came to an end to be replaced by a
Commendator. From the time David I had raised the
Church of the Holy Trinity to the dignity of an Abbey in
1124 to January 1560 there had been recorded 36 Abbots.
Robert Pitcairn became Commendator in 1560, though he
is named as Abbot in his monumental tomb in the Abbey
nave.

Some thought had also been paid to the problem of
preserving the relics of St Margaret and they had been
moved for safe-keeping to Edinburgh Castle. At this point
it might be of interest to relate the future fate of these relics.

When Edinburgh Castle fell into the hands of the
Reformers the coffer containing the skull was secretly
conveyed to the manor-house of the Laird of Dury who had
been the last Abbot of Dunfermline and who kept this
religious treasure for many years. To quote Father Hay in
his Scotia Sacra it was in 1597 delivered into the hands of
the Jesuit missionaries in Scotland, who, seeing it was in

danger of being lost or profaned transferred it to Antwerp where John Malderus, bishop of the city, after diligent examination upon oath, gave an authenticity under the seal of his office, 5th September 1620 and permitted it to be exposed to the observation of the people. The same relic was acknowledged by Paul Bindot, bishop of Arras, 4th September 1627 in testimony of which he offered forty days indulgence to all who would pray before it. Lastly, on March the fourth, 1640, Pope Innocent X gave plenary indulgence to all the faithful who would pray before it, having confessed or communicated in the chapel of the Scots College at Douai. The saint's relics were kept in the Scots College in a bust of silver, her skull enclosed in the head of the bust, on which there was a crown of silver gilt, enriched with several pearls and precious stones. In the pedestal, which was of ebony indented with silver, her hair was kept and exposed to the view of everyone through a glass of crystal. There were likewise several stones, red and green, in the breast and shoulders. I cannot tell if they be real — their bigness makes me fancy they may be counterfeit.

These relics disappeared during the time of the French Revolution.

It is easy to imagine the mixed feelings with which the citizens of Dunfermline witnessed the desecration of their Abbey when the lords and barons with fanatical followers paused on their way to Stirling and 'kest it doun.' Some would sincerely lament the sacrilege or mourn the loss of the trade brought to the town by the Abbey's patronage while others would warmly approve of the deeds of the Reformers, hoping to escape from ancient tyrannies and outmoded prejudices. They had all been brought up in fear and respect of the power of the Church, whatever their later doubts, and it must have been with incredulous awe that they witnessed its ruin. The High altars, with twenty other altars, images, painted saints, inscribed tablets, shrines, effigies, tombs, crosses, vestments, saints' relics and handbells — everything was brought out into the open, broken up and set on fire. The western tower may have suffered because it contained the baptised bells and with it

Dunfermline Abbey and Palace ruins from Pittencrieff Park

fell part of the west gable. It was, however, to the eastern part of the Abbey that the Reformers mostly directed their attention for in the Choir were stationed the main altars and shrines. The nave survived because it had always served as the parish-church. As usual the broken walls of Abbey and monastery served through the years as a quarry for building materials and at one time many sculptured stones were to be found in the walls of domestic dwellings. Now only the south wall of the refectory remains and it is difficult to imagine how the place must have looked before it became a parish graveyard.

All over the country the widespread possessions of the Abbey passed into other hands. Revenues from places like Dunkeld, Moulin, Perth, Scone, Pluscardin, Pettycur, Berwick, Cleish, Dollar, Tillicoultrie, Linlithgow and Stirling were lost, together with the patronage of countless churches, chapels and hospices. There had been about twenty altars in the Abbey — the High Altar, Our Lady's Altar, the Haly-Bluid Altar, the Rood Altar in company with others dedicated to various saints, John, Peter, James, Thomas, Michael, Salvator, Laurence, Margaret, Ninian, Nicholas, Cuthbert, Stephen, Catharine and the Paris Altar.

The resignation of the Abbey lands in the neighbourhood meant considerable additions to the properties of local lairds, like the Wellwoods and the Halketts, with farms and mills passing into the hands of farmers at Touch, Baldridge, Grange and North Fod.

Four months after the attack on the Abbey in 1560 David Ferguson was appointed the first Protestant minister there. It is thought he was born in Dundee, a glover by trade, and became an early preacher of the reformed doctrines to all those who would listen to him. He was given the charge at Dunfermline by the newly-appointed General Assembly and though he entered upon the work with enthusiasm his stipend was meagre and he, along with many of his fellow-ministers, had to depend a good deal upon the charity of his congregation. He was thrice Moderator of the General Assembly which he represented on many important occasions. In 1572, at a meeting of the Assembly at Leith, he preached a rousing sermon before the Regent Mar, protesting against the spoils of the Roman Catholic Church going to the private uses of the nobility instead of being applied to the building of schools and churches and helping those in need. The speech was printed and warmly commended by John Knox.

David Ferguson had a pleasant sense of humour, good manners and was frequently sent to the King when there were matters of importance to discuss especially when the vexed question of bishops in Scotland was raised. He married Isobel Durham and had nine children — five sons and four daughters — and he died in Dunfermline in April 1589, at the age of sixty-five years 'having laboured in the ministry for thirty-eight years.'

But in spite of David Ferguson and his enthusiasm for the Reformed religion, Dunfermline had lost its Abbey and all that it meant to the community in fame and importance. The Palace, however, remained, and it was on the future Royal favour that the citizens hopefully relied.

6
Royal Visits

At this point it might be as well to gather together such details as are known of the royal visits to the Palace, which, enlarged and refurbished for the pleasure of James the Fifth's French wife, now entered upon a new lease of life. The Palace yard which had once been the Abbey Close echoed to the coming and going of mounted escorts. Blazing logs and coal in the great fireplaces filled the thick-walled rooms with heat and light, the long southern windows looked out upon a pastoral scene with well-tilled fields beyond the trees of Pittencrieff. Fish could be caught in the burn; there were coneys, red squirrels, boars and game birds in the surrounding woods and the spacious kitchens of the Palace would be full of activity as lavish meals were prepared by crude enough methods for the banquets in the great hall.

On her return to Scotland in 1561 Queen Mary visited the Palace on various occasions, one of which was to avoid the attentions of M. Châtelard, grand-nephew of the famous Bayard. The persistence of this gentleman in trying to force his way into the Queen's bedroom came to an abrupt end when he was arrested at Burntisland and later executed at St Andrews. When the Queen escaped from Lochleven Castle, she and her train of gentlemen passed through the east end of the town, but they were in a hurry to cross the Forth and did not linger. Not long after, Mary left Scotland, never to return, and the next royal visitor to the Palace was her son James, a shambling youth of eighteen who rode over from Linlithgow with the earls of

Argyle, Angus, Montrose, Bothwell, Marischal and Marr in his company.

James must have taken a liking to the Palace for he frequently returned there. It was the meeting-place chosen for his conference with the Danish Ambassadors who, speaking in Latin, urged their country's claim to the islands of Orkney and Shetland, saying they were ready to begin negotiations. Later James at St Andrews, promised to find out the truth of the matter and sent back an answer to Denmark by one of his councillors. Nothing more was heard about this till the islands were named as part of the dowry of his consort, Anne of Denmark.

When James came of age in 1588 he granted a Confirmation Charter to the Burgh of Dunfermline, confirming the gifts and privileges conferred on the Burgh by three of the Abbots — Robert in 1322, John in 1305 and George in 1549. This has sometimes been taken to mean that James was constituting Dunfermline as a Royal Burgh, which was done long before by Alexander I in the twelfth century and this Charter is a Charter of Confirmation, not one of Erection. It is to be found in the Charter Chest of the Burgh together with an English translation and confirms not only the boundaries of the town, mentioning the common muir, the great moss and the various marches but all the liberties, gifts, privileges, made by the King and Church throughout the centuries. The witnesses of the Charter, signed by the King at Holyrood, included Lord Hamilton, the Earl of Angus, and Sir John Maitland of Thirlstane, Chancellor and Secretary.

This Charter may have done much to calm the indignation that must have been aroused in the town by the King's high-handed decision to strip the Church of its properties and add them to the Crown. The Abbey of Dunfermline lost the lands and lordship of Musselburgh, although the Estates added an exception by which the livings, pensions and duties of the Abbey were not to be affected during the beneficiaries' lifetime. The King also granted Dunfermline the right to hold public fairs on March 1st and the 10th September, later adding July 20th and October 22nd with permission to collect tolls and customs from the same.

James' interest in Dunfermline was further demonstrated by the 'morning gift' he made to Anne of Denmark on the morning of their marriage at Upsala in Norway in 1589 which was the Lordship of Dunfermline.

The Lordship of Dunfermline then meant the lands and revenues belonging to the Abbey which had been excepted from the general annexation of Church property to be given to the Crown in 1587. This grant was confirmed in 1593 by two Acts of the Scottish Parliament entitled 'Act of the new gift of Dunfermline with the monks' portions to the Queen's Majesty,' and 'Act concerning the Queen's Majesty's right to the third of Dunfermline and compensation for much as presently wants thereof.' As stated in the former the Queen was to enjoy said gift 'for all the days in her lifetime' which probably meant that she was to benefit from the property while she lived, independently of the King, while a clause in the second held her to pay a silver penny at the feast of Whit Sunday as an acknowledgement of vassalage to the Crown.

Her possession of the lordship, according to this Act, embraced all the baronies and lands within it, together with 'mansions, houses, castles, towns, fortalices and manor-places', in which, though it was not specifically mentioned, the Palace was probably included. Her part of the Palace which consisted of a house standing in the forecourt of the Palace could not have been in very good shape as William Schaw, the King's Master of Works, received £400 by order of His Majesty to repair the place which James later inspected before the arrival of the Queen about the twelfth of July 1590. Their Majesties apparently enjoyed their sojourns at the Palace, as, in the next few years, they were there on several occasions. After her investment in the lordship Queen Anne used the title of Lady of Dunfermline in any matters connected with the town and it was in the Palace that she gave birth to three of her children — Elizabeth who was the ancestress of the present Queen, Charles who became King as Charles I and Robert who only lived a few months and was buried in a vault in the Abbey. Curiously enough, this vault was given by the King and Queen to Sir Henry Wardlaw of Pitreavie in 1616.

When James brought his bride back from Norway various ships had to be provided for the expedition — two from Edinburgh, assisted by Kinghorn and Inverkeithing, one ship from Ayr with help from Rothesay, Dumbarton, Renfrew, Rutherglen, Irvine and Glasgow. One from St Andrews, assisted by Dunfermline, Burntisland, Kirkcaldy, Dysart, Pittenweem. One ship from Dundee, assisted by Arbroath and Forfar, one ship from Aberdeen, assisted by Brechin, Elgin, Inverness. These ships were to be brought to the Firth of Forth between 13th March and 1st April, 1590. They crossed the North Sea to escort the King and his bride back to Scotland where they landed at Leith on May 1st.

At the close of the century there seemed to be a good deal of building going on in St Catharine's Wynd. In 1599 two houses were built by the west side of the old church steeple, as residences for the High Constable, Sergeant and Heritable Bailie of the Regality of Dunfermline and not far off a new Queen's House was erected on the site of the older one. This was a strange building of three storeys with a pend running through it to connect it with the Palace yard. Over the south key-stone of the pend a large sheet of copper displayed a Latin inscription of which the following is a rough translation — 'This porch and the house built above it, having through age and the injuries of time fallen down and come to ruin, have been restored from the foundations and on a larger scale by Queen Anne, daughter of Frederick, the most august King of Denmark, in the year 1600.' Perhaps when the Court was in residence at the Palace, Anne liked to escape to the less formal atmosphere of this house where she could indulge her passion for dancing and skipping. After all, at the time of her·marriage she was only fifteen years old and very attractive with a dazzlingly fair complexion, blue eyes and long golden hair. At first James was very much in love with her and it was only later that he discovered she was also very obstinate and rather stupid.

The name of William Schaw, Master of Works, has been

mentioned in connection with the work he did for Anne on her house. He was something of a genius where building was concerned and when he was put in charge of the restoration of the Abbey he set about erecting the steeple and the north porch, some of the buttresses, the roofs of the north and south aisles and part of the west gable above the great western door. On his death in Dunfermline in 1602 he was buried in the north aisle of the nave where his impressive monument stated in Latin that 'among the living he dwelt fifty-two years; he had travelled in France and many other kingdoms for the improvement of his mind; he wanted for no liberal training; was most skilful as an architect; was early recommended to great persons for the singular gifts of his mind and was not only unwearied and undefatigable in labours and business but constantly active and vigorous and was most dear to every man who knew him. He was born to do good offices and thereby to gain the hearts of men; now he lives eternally with God. Queen Anne ordered this monument to be erected to the memory of this most excellent and upright man, lest his virtues, worthy of eternal commendation, should pass away with the death of his body.'

It is perhaps just as well that the Queen could not foresee the future treatment of this monument. In 1794 it was removed from its site behind the pulpit pillar to the foot of the steeple as the minister needed a larger window made in the north wall to throw more light on his Bible. It is a pity that the Department of Works which is responsible cannot afford to throw a little more light on this interesting relic from the past which is allowed to moulder away in the darkest corner of the nave.

In 1603, on Queen Elizabeth's death, James succeeded to the Crown of England and for Dunfermline with the departure of the Court to London another chapter in the history of its Royal Palace came to an end. The building was left in the charge of Henry Wardlaw, her Majesty's Chamberlain, and Lord Seton, who as tutor to Prince Charles, resided for some time in the Palace before taking his charge south to England. James, when he left, solemnly promised in a speech to the people in the great Kirk of

Edinburgh, to return to his northern kingdom every three years, but it was a promise he did not keep and nearly fourteen years were to elapse before he saw Scotland again.

In 1617 there came news of a proposed visit of King James which threw the whole Privy Council into a panic. The Palaces of Holyroodhouse and Dunfermline had to be repaired and made ready for the King's accommodation and all other employment must wait. Masons, burgesses and craftsmen were directed to other work immediately. 'They shall be kindly treated and weel usit and shall receive honest and thankful payment for their services under pain or rebellion and putting to the horn.' Tremendous preparations were made to cope with His Majesty's baggage which could amount to some thirty-five cartloads. Fife was divided into four precincts. The plewlands (ploughlands) were counted and one horse assessed against each 'plew'. A general Constable was chosen for every district and a particular Constable for each parish. In the precincts of the Presbytery of Dunfermline everything was carefully arranged and the whole parish certified to provide thirty horses. The King was received with 'tumultous joy' wherever he appeared and he made two visits to Dunfermline, in May and in June, staying a few days each time.

In July, 1633 there is an interesting glimpse of a royal occasion for Charles I, touring Scotland, came back to the place of his birth and there 'with great solemnitie about nine of the clock on Friday in the morning,' Sir Robert Kerr of Ancrum, knight-gentleman of His Majesty's bedchamber and keeper of his privy-purse, was created Earl of Ancrum, Lord Kerr of Nesbit, Longnewton and Dolphinton. He was brought into the King's presence between the Earl of Morton on the right hand and Charles, Earl of Dunfermline, on his left. His robes were borne by Ross Herald, his coronet by Islay and his patent by Lyon King of Arms. In His Majesty's presence he was proclaimed by Lyon who administered the oath and this was read by the Clerk of the Council in the Secretary's absence. The heralds went to the windows of the great chamber and sounded their trumpets as proclamation. The tables for the King's guests were laid out for a large company in the

Fraters' Hall, across the way.

On the same occasion Charles dubbed five knights and Alexander Clerk of Pittencrieff may have been one of them. It was in this year, also, that Thomas Bruce, third Lord Kinloss, was created Earl of Elgin by the King, while, at Dalkeith, James Halkett of Pitfirrane was knighted.

The next royal visit to the Palace was not quite so pleasant. Charles the Second who, on the execution of his father, had yet to enter into his inheritance, came to Scotland and to Dunfermline where he signed the document known as the Dunfermline Declaration, in which he renounced Popery and Prelacy, vowing that he would have 'no friends but the friends of the Covenant, no enemies but the enemies of the Covenant, that he would always esteem them as servants and most loyal subjects and give unto God the things that are God's and to Ceasar the things that are Caesar's.'

He was at the time a rather impatient and arrogant young man of twenty, heartily bored by the sermons he had had to endure and Mr. Patrick Gillespie who put the pen in his hand, seemed to have had some doubts as to his sincerity. He told the King that if he were not satisfied in his soul as to the righteousness of his signing the document he should not hesitate to say so. But Charles impatiently replied 'Mr. Gillespie, Mr. Gillespie, I am satisfied, I am satisfied and therefore will subscribe to it.' History was to show how little weight he placed upon these solemn promises.

Charles was crowned at Scone on the first of January, 1651, and then set out on a tour of Scotland, visiting Perth, Falkland, Dundee, Stirling, lodging for a night at the Palace of Wemyss, with the laird of Anstruther and the Earl of Crawford at Struthers. He was twice more in the Palace of Dunfermline and on the latter of these occasions one of those presented to the King was Miss Ann Murray, daughter of a former Provost of Eton. It was not their first meeting, for Ann had been appointed by Charles First and Queen Henrietta as governess to the Duke of Gloucester and the Princess Elizabeth, Charles' younger brother and sister. After the death of Charles the First Ann sought refuge in Scotland and was at this time staying with her friends the Earl and Countess of Dunfermline who presented her to the King. He did not apparently realise her connection with his family and it was only after, being somewhat affronted, she had persuaded one of his entourage to prompt the royal memory that Charles, on the morning of his departure, spoke more personally to her. In Ann's own words 'he turned to me and said "Mistress Murray, I am ashamed I should be so long a'speaking to you but it was because I could not say enough to you for the service you did my brother; but if ever I can command what I have a right to, as my own, there shall be nothing in my power that I will not do for you."'

No doubt this was said with his usual charm and left her feeling gratified by his interest. But apparently she did nothing to remind the King of his promise. She was married to Sir James Halkett of Pitfirrane and spent twenty-eight years of her widowhood in the old house that was once called the Commendator's, known now as the Abbots. Here she wrote a score of books on religious meditation and died at last on the twenty-second of April 1699 at what was then the advanced age of seventy-seven, a span of years that covered all the troubled history of England and Scotland, during the reigns of James VI and I, Charles I, Cromwell, Charles II, James VII and II, William and Mary, with all the trials and troubles of religious persecutions. But maybe, secure in the shelter of the old stone house, she was only interested in the writing of her pious reflections, looking out of the window at the Abbey and the graveyard where in the end she would be buried.

Dunfermline Abbey Tower framed in a window of the Palace ruins

7
Local Landowners

As very few local people seem to have heard of the Earl of Dunfermline this might be a good moment to explain how this title came into being and also to describe other long-established families living in the district. Born in 1550, Alexander Seton was the third surviving son of Isobel Hamilton by Lord Seton, faithful friend to Queen Mary. Queen Mary was Alexander's god-mother and for a Bairn's gift she presented him with the lands of Pluscardine in Moray. As a youth he was sent to Rome with the idea of making a Churchman of him and he resided for some time in the Jesuit college there. However, probably realising how the Reformation was going to change things, he decided to study canon and civil law instead and after staying in France, studying, for about seven years, he returned to Scotland. There he was called to the Bar, probably about 1577, and he accompanied his father on an Embassy to France in 1586. Just before this, Seton was named an Extraordinary Lord of Session (1585) by the style of Baron of Pluscardine, the property having been confirmed .to him twenty years before by Mary and Darnley. On his return from France he was created an ordinary Lord of Session under the title or style of Lord Meldrum of Seggie on the death of James Meldrum. At that time he was still suspected of being a Catholic and was obliged to take Communion at a time fixed by the ministers in Edinburgh.

In 1591 he was raised to the Peerage of Scotland by the title of Lord Fyvie and in May 1593 he was appointed

President of Session in succession to President Baillie, becoming Baron Fyvie on the 14th May 1597. He had charge of the education of the King's second son, who became Charles the First, till the Court removed to England in 1603. Fyvie Castle went with the title and it became for a time Alexander's favourite residence. There had been a building on this site on the Ythan's left bank for centuries. Edward the First of England had stayed there in 1296 when it was a royal seat. In 1380 the Earl of Carrick, later Robert III, had made it over to his cousin, Sir James de Lindsay. The next owner was Sir Henry Preston, his brother-in-law, and then, for over a hundred years it had been the home of the Meldrums from whom Alexander acquired it in 1596. He made many important alterations to the impressive pile, adding a splendid double-tower to the centre of the south front. In appearance and furnishings the Castle soon resembled a French chateau and it must have made a splendid home for Alexander and his first wife, Lilias, second daughter of Patrick, third Lord Drummond, a plump handsome young woman 'with a merry smile.'

Alexander was high in the King's favour and he was asked to superintend the education of Prince Henry and later of Prince Charles, who came as a baby to the nursery at Fyvie Castle where he joined in the play with Alexander's children. These were a disappointment to him for he had five daughters and no son. This disappointment must have been equally trying for his wife Lilias. After ten years of constant child-bearing no doubt she had lost her 'merry smile', and by 1601 she was dead. Owing to his powerful family connections Alexander was able to arrange good matches for his daughters — Anne to Alexander, Viscount Fenton, only son of the first Earl of Kelso, Isobel to John, first Earl of Lauderdale, Margaret to Colin, first Earl of Seaforth and Sophia to David, first Lord Lindsay of Balcarres.

After Lilias' death Alexander, still anxious for sons, lost no time in finding her successor and six months later he married Grizel Lindsay, fourth daughter of James Leslie, Master of Rothes. At last a son was born and two more daughters, Lilias who remained unmarried and Jean who became the wife of John, the eighth Lord Yester. But, sad to say, the son died of plague as a child and his mother did not long survive him. Two years later, when he was fifty-five, Alexander married Margaret Hay, sister of John, first earl of Tweeddale. She was just fifteen years old. There were two more daughters and at last a son Charles who lived to inherit his father's titles and became the second Earl of Dunfermline.

On her marriage to James, Queen Anne had received from him as 'a morning's gift' the lordship of Dunfermline and this, in 1596, the Queen conferred upon Alexander, together with the Heritable Ballieship of the Regality Court of Dunfermline. This was an ancient office, instituted by Robert the Bruce in 1322, along with letters patent and a Coquet Seal which was the authority for collecting these customs granted by the King to the Abbey. After the Reformation the office of Bailie became heritable and was held by David Durie who resigned the office and all its perquisites into the Queen's hands. When she bestowed it on Alexander, he was able to collect mails of money from all the feu-farms and other duties formerly payable to the Monastery from all the lands belonging to it on the north side of the Forth, together with free entertainment for himself 'twelve followers, horse and foot, in meat and drink and suitable lodging and accommodation' while he was attending the three-yearly head-courts and other courts of the Regality for the administration of justice. What was even more important, Alexander also obtained the title of Heritable Admiral of the whole lordship of Dunfermline except Musselburgh, resigned to the Earl of Dunfermline by Ludovick, Duke of Lennox Great Admiral of Scotland. This gave him the 'right title and possession of all the ships and sea-wracks accidents and casualties of all lands, seas, waters and others pertaining to the said lordship of Dunfermline upon both sides of the Forth.'

It would seem from this that Alexander was on to a good thing. He had little to do to collect these perquisites but he apparently did not like staying in Dunfermline, deserted by the Court after the move to England. For, early in his bailieship, he exchanged his right of free accommodation there for 'a grant of ten chalders of black oats yearly and the whole kain of capon and poultry of the lordship.'

About this time, though he probably spent much of his time in England, he was preparing Pinkie House near Musselburgh for his occupation. It was a country mansion that had belonged to the Abbots of Dunfermline and was completed with the creation of a Painted Gallery, where heraldic emblems gleamed in red and blue and gold, and an impressive chamber was called the King's room. The two young Princes Henry and Charles are supposed to have spent three years of their childhood in Pinkie House before going to England.

Above the front door he put an inscription in Latin:—

'Lord Alexander Seton built this house not after the fashion of his mind but after that of his fortune and estates. 1613.'

Following the murder of the Earl of Moray in February, 1591-92, Alexander, then Lord Urquhart, had bought the house and property of Dalgety from the former owners. Lying on the north side of the Forth, this estate was easily accessible from both land and sea, and as he grew older and perhaps feebler, Alexander liked to retire to the 'small low house,' which offered him a refuge from the affairs of state, living there with his young wife and precious son, no doubt frequently visited by his numerous daughters and their families. He had built an imposing vault in the little chapel at Dalgety and it was to this vault that, after his death in Pinkie House in 1622, his body was brought on one July day.

He had expressly forbidden any show of pomp and circumstance but it was an imposing procession that made its way across the Forth in barges and through the woods to Dalgety. There were men-at-arms and pursuivants 'in rich apparel, lackeys clad in dule, trumpeters, standard-bearers, attendants holding aloft Alexander's achieve-ments, emblazoned on richly-painted shields' while others bore the robes of the dead Lord Chancellor, the Great Seal and Mace covered with black crepe. Alexander's brothers carried his sword and his belt, his coronet on a red cushion, following after the coffin which was of timber, covered by a mortcloth of black velvet under a black velvet canopy. Another gold coronet rested at the head.

Many of the great men of Scotland and England were there, richly clad, their trains held up by attendants, and as there was room only for a small company in the chapel, most of them waited outside in the sunshine till the service was over. It was an impressive tribute paid by his peers to a man who had won respect by his courage, honesty and wit.

But, as is frequently the case when men carve out an impressive career for themselves, gaining respect and admiration as well as wealth, Alexander Seton's descendants did nothing to enhance the family's reputation. The second earl at first supported the National Covenant but later became a strong Royalist, the fourth earl fought at Killiecrankie for James VII and died without issue, an attainted exile at St Germain's in 1694. It was the end of an old song that, for the Seton family, had lasted only ninety years as earls of Dunfermline.

One of the oldest of the local families was the Stewarts of Rosyth who claimed to be of royal descent from James, fifth High Steward of Scotland. The family's numerous descendants included the Angus Stewarts, the Earls of Lennox and the Earl of Galloway who was the ancestor of the Stewarts of Innerneath, Lorne, Durisdeer and Grandtully. Sir Robert Stewart of Durrisdeer fell at the battle of Shrewsbury in 1409, leaving, with other children, a son and daughter Isobel who was married to Sir Robert Bruce of Clackmannan, from whom the Earls of Elgin, the Bruces of Airth and the Bruces of Earlshall were all descended. Sir David Stewart, her brother, became the first Stewart of Rosyth and was knighted at the coronation of James I in May 1424. Before he purchased Rosyth he possessed other properties in Fife and in 1428 he had the whole of them, including Pitreavie, formed into a free barony of Rosyth. He died in 1444.

His grandson David was one of the barons in the Parliament of 1467. His daughter Janet was married to Alan Bruce of Earlshall and became the mother of the famous Sir William Bruce (1486-1584) who built Earlshall and was buried in Leuchars Kirk. His son David married Margaret, daughter of Sir Robert Douglas of Lochleven. In 1488 he founded a chaplaincy at the altar of St Michael Archangel in the Parish Church of Inverkeithing. As he had no surviving issue, Sir David granted a charter of Rosyth to his uncle William Stewart of Briery-hill who came into possession of Rosyth in 1492. His descendants held Rosyth for the next two hundred years. He was followed by his son in 1514 so it is probable that he fell at Flodden with his King.

Another ancient family with a long local connection was the Halketts of Pitfirrane. The name had been traced back to David de Hackett who was proprietor of the lands of Ballingall in the days of David II, and his grandson, who bore the same name, was designated 'of Pitfirrane' in a charter of 1437. At that time there was a dwelling on the site of the present mansion which was altered and extended by George Halkett who succeeded to the estate in 1573. A panel in the staircase dated 1583 was believed to be the date of these alterations.

George Halkett was Provost of Dunfermline in 1585 when the town 'being free of the pest' was chosen as a meeting-place of the General Assembly before Parliament. This meeting was countermanded by the King and it was on his orders that the Provost caused the town-ports to be closed. The Assembly met in a field outside the town and agreed to meet in Linlithgow at a later date. James Melville, that diligent diarist, added a curious postscript to his account of the affair.

'But God within a few years payit that laird and provost his hire for that piece of service, when, for the halding out of His servants from keiping His Assemblie in that toun, he made his awin house to spew him out; for on a day in the morning, he was fallen out of a window in his awin house of Pitfirren, three or four houses hight; whether by a melancholy despair, casting himself, or by the violence of unkynd guests lodged within, God Knaws; for, being taken up, his speech was not so sensible as to declare it but within a few hours after deit.'

To continue with the list of local landowners, Broomhall is the family seat of the Earl of Elgin and Kincardine. This estate is situated between Limekilns and Dunfermline and in the beginning, under the name Gedeleth, corrupted to Gellett, it belonged to the Monastery of Dunfermline. Wester Gellett was purchased about 1600 by Sir George Bruce of Carnock who changed the name to Broomhall and gave the estate to his second son Robert Bruce who was made a Lord of Session in 1649 with the title of Lord Broomhall. The history of this family is too complicated to deal with here in detail but over the centuries the name of Elgin and Kincardine has gathered fame and distinction. Thomas, seventh Earl of Elgin and eleventh Earl of Kincardine brought the Elgin Marbles to the British Museum when he was Ambassador to Constantinople. His son, James, was Governor-General of Jamaica, Canada and India in turn. The mansion-house of Broomhall, built upon the site of an earlier building, overlooks the Firth of Forth with the model village of Charlestown, created in 1761 by the Earl for his workers in the nearby lime-works, at the end of one of the avenues.

Another well known family, the Wardlaws of Pitreavie, claimed that their ancestors had come from Saxony into England in the sixth century, receiving estates in Galloway which were granted to them by Malcolm Canmore when they followed him into Scotland at the time of the Norman Conquest. Later they obtained lands at Torrie in Tor-rieburn and though they supported the cause of Balliol and lost their other estates, Sir Henry Wardlaw of Torrie was sufficiently liked and trusted by the Bruce to be given in marriage the daughter of Walter, the High Steward of Scotland. Other branches of the family settled in Luscar and Sir Cuthbert Wardlaw of Balmule had as his eldest son and heir Henry Wardlaw, born 1565, who afterwards became Sir Henry Wardlaw of Pitreavie and Balmule. He was popular in Court circles and was appointed Chamberlain to Anne of Denmark, King James' Queen. Married to Elizabeth Hutton, he had five sons and three daughters whose marriages brought a wideflung family connection with other landed families. In 1615 Sir Henry Wardlaw built the Castle of Pitreavie, a substantial mansion with two symmetrical wings on either side of the main building, its three or four storeys crowned by large chimney-stacks and steep slated roofs and pointed turrets. On the first floor, reached by a handsomely-carved staircase, the rooms connected with each other in the French fashion but on the floor above, the bedrooms had separate doors and opened directly off the staircase. There have, of course, been many alterations in the Castle since Henry Wardlaw's time, the greatest being the building of an underground communication-centre and weather-station before the second World War, but the old house still stands among the trees and plants which Henry Beveridge, who lived there with his family about the end of last century, brought back from his travels abroad.

The estate of the Hill, to the south of Dunfermline, was acquired in 1621 by William Monteith of Randleford. The date 1623 was carved below the front window. It is probable that as some details of architecture and ornamentation resemble the work Inigo Jones did on the Hospital of George Heriot in Edinburgh this famous architect was employed on the house. He was in Denmark with King James VI and his Queen, returned to Scotland with them and probably stayed for some time in the Palace when he may have had a hand in designing the Queen's House. In the Hill House there are various inscriptions in Hebrew and Latin, together with different initials, and carved figures supposed to represent King David and King James found on the stairs and over the windows, together with the emblems of Scotland, England, Ireland and Wales. Since William Monteith's time the house and estate have had many different owners.

8
The Great Fire

So, with the coming of the seventeenth century, Dunfermline found it had lost a good deal of its former importance.

Its citizens had grown accustomed to seeing the Royal family at worship in the restored nave of the Abbey which was now the parochial church, the Princes and Princesses at play in the gardens of the Palace. Court ladies had patronised the booths in the narrow streets and a blacksmith's forge, established in the shadow of the Monastery walls to make horse-shoes for all couriers and men-at-arms who came and went on the King's business, now had to rely on the custom of farmers coming to market or travellers passing through on their way to other places. Many of the merchants became bankrupt and, with no tenants in the principal shops, people in search in clothing, books or some special item of food had to travel to Culross which was then a flourishing port on the Forth.

The houses that had lodged the French and Danish Ambassadors stood empty and the King's stables were removed, while a few servants eked out a forgotten and rather precarious existence among the deserted rooms of the Palace which were, with difficulty, kept wind and water tight. It all come back to life with the escape of their majesties from the Papist plot to murder them with gunpowder. Their return was celebrated with a musical entertainment and there were bonfires and tar-barrels burning on the streets, with bells ringing and prayers in the Kirk.

A few furtive pilgrims might still visit St Margaret's

ruined Shrine and cave but they were not encouraged. The reformed religion had turned its back on such superstitious behaviour and in the restored nave of the Abbey congregations listened with dour attention to the stern behests of their ministers of the Gospel, Mr John Fairford and Mr Andro Foster, standing about among the massive pillars where once resplendent Lord-Abbots had led their attendant trains of great churchmen and princes of the blood royal. Maybe, in spite of the draughts that had blown through the broken windows, a breath of incense still lingered in the air.

The alienation of the Abbey lands went on. By various Charters John Scobie obtained the lands of Wester Luscar, Sir Robert Halkett of Pitfirrane the teind sheaves of Bairdleys, six miles north-west of the town; James Reid the croft acres of Dunfermline; Alexander, Earl of Dunfermline, the coal in the Lordship of Dunfermline with the fourth part of North Fod; Robert Peirson the lands of Nether Beath and Robert Halkett the mill of Pitliver. Sir Henry Wardlaw was granted the lands of Pitbauchlie with the teind sheaves of Pitreavie.

The town, however, was not entirely forgotten by the Queen. In 1610 Queen Anne commanded through Sir Henry Wardlaw the mortification of £2000 Scots, the annual rent of which was to form a Fund for a salary to the Master of the Grammar and Song School of Dunfermline. The title of Master of the Song School is the legal definition of this post and requires that the person elected should teach a Song School in the town. The last holder of the office was the late Mr James Moodie, musical director of the Carnegie Dunfermline Trust.

About this time a Royal gallery was erected in the nave of the Abbey church between two pillars opposite the pulpit. It was intended for the use of the royal family but in fact it remained empty for seven years till King James' visit in 1617. This gallery was decorated with the Crowns of Scotland and Denmark in gilt, with the initials of James and his Queen. Over the seat was a Latin inscription 'Cum Deum Cogitas, Qui Dat Vitam et Necessarie.'

To the west was another gallery built for the Earl of

Dunfermline, which was also lavishly decorated with coronets and Latin inscriptions. The Earl's coat-of-arms with its shields, crescents, mullets and white horses was displayed on a board in front of the seat. The Magistrates' gallery was to the right of the pulpit.

In the early years of the century there was plenty for the citizens to gossip about. A new port at the top of Rotten Row, an earthquake that shook all Fife, the final touches put to the repairing of the Abbey nave by the Earl of Dunfermline whose initials appear on a stone at the side of the south-porch door with the date 1607.

There was also the strange affair in 1616 of the minister Andro Foster or Forrester who, having appropriated money from the poor-box, experienced a sudden repentance or fear of arrest 'being seized with such horror that he ran out of the pulpit, requesting Mr Murray for Christ's sake, to take charge of the congregation.' It was in his time a cross or crucifix was painted upon the Earl of Dunfermline's seat in the church and the minister was blamed for allowing this.

Another scandal of the period concerned John Wemyss of Pittencrieff who was excommunicated for the murder of his natural brother and had to present himself on five successive Sundays clad in sackcloth, to make public repentance of his sin in the churches of Kirkcaldy, Dysart, Cupar, St Andrews and Dunfermline.

In 1610 Sir Alexander Clark of Pennicuik was building a mansion-house of severely plain design set deep in the heart of his Pittencrieff estate. At one time the rent of this property, lately owned by the Earl of Dunfermline and belonging to the Crown, was a red rose on the day of the feast of the Blessed Virgin.

In 1618 Dunfermline was visited by two celebrated men of letters. Ben Jonson arrived on foot in August to be followed in September of the same year by John Taylor 'the Water Poet' who described himself as a penniless pedestrian and wrote a book on his adventures. In Dunfermline he was entertained by a certain 'Master John Gibb, Groom of His Majesty's Chambers, and a goodly company of local gentlemen, both Scots and English.'

Pittencrieff House

It seems that after Queen Anne's death in 1619 part of her lordship of Dunfermline passed to her son Charles, which would no doubt gratify the citizens and was to be of some importance in the town's future.

For there came a day in May, 1624 when the whole existence of the town was threatened by fire. The twenty-fifth of May was Wappinshaw Day when all the able-bodied male citizens were summoned to parade with their weapons and it seems that in the yard of a house near Rotten Row, young Willie Anderson, son of Baillie Anderson, with his servant Charles Richeson and some of his young friends, was firing his gun when a wad of burning lint fell upon the thatch of a nearby house. The wind, blowing strongly from the north-west, fanned the flames and in four hours the fire had burned a wide path through the town from the Rotten Row to the Nethertown, destroying the houses in Collier Row (Bruce Street) north Chapel Street, the Crosswynd, all the north and part of the south side of the High Street, the upper part of the New

Row and the north side of the Maygate. The Abbey was fortunately beyond the reach of the flames but it seems that the Tolbooth may have been damaged as the house next-door to it, also curiously owned by an Anderson, was completely destroyed. In spite of all the efforts of the citizens about nine-tenths of the town was burned down. Most of the houses with wooden upper storeys above a stone ground floor were thatched with turf or heather or straw and burned like tinder. People did what they could to save their belongings and live-stock and there is no report that anyone perished in the flames, but it was calculated that two hundred and twenty 'tenements' housing two hundred and eighty-seven families were totally destroyed along with five hundred bools of meal in store.

A curious feature of the tragedy is that there is no mention of it in the Burgh records of that date and there were only a few later references to the disbursing of funds received. Several Scottish burghs collected voluntary contributions in money and goods, among the first being Aberdeen which sent 1600 merks. Some time after this, in July, Edinburgh Town Council handed over to Robert Drummond and James Reid, Burgesses of Dunfermline, the collected sum of four thousand, five hundred pounds (Scots) eight shillings and sevenpence to help with the re-building of the town. The Lords of the Privy Council wrote a long appeal for help to James VI and to Prince Charles 'because it is his ain toun.' The amount of the King's benevolence is not known but Prince Charles sent the Provost five hundred pounds. The amounts are all in Scots money which by this time was worth only a twelfth of sterling.

This fire explains why there are so few old houses in the centre part of the town and how the mansion now called the Abbot's House alone survived from the fifteenth century, presenting, with its crow-stepped gables, massive walls and steeply pitched roofs, an example of what some other buildings might have looked like before the street was destroyed.

One of the casualties of the fire was the town's Grammar School which had come into being soon after the destruction of the Abbey. A new building was erected on the same site on the south side of Queen Anne Street, a modest affair of two storeys with an outside stair built on to the east gable. Above doors and windows were carved various apposite texts — 'Favour me, o my God.' 'Often teach and chastise that the boy may live.' 'Learn and suffer. Thus thy God shall bless thee.' The town arms and the date 1625 accompanied these admonishments. The school was soon found to be too small and various alterations and additions were made before it was supplanted by a larger and more handsome building in 1817.

Those of the citizens who could afford the expense immediately began to rebuild their houses but it was not until the end of the year, when some of the public contributions were paid out, that the real rebuilding of the town got under way, with stone-masons, carpenters and slaters busy with saw, hammer and chisel. It seems that the Burgesses of Dunfermline had the right to cut wood on the estate of Garvock, a heavily-wooded hill to the east of the town, and they made such demands on the trees there that the proprietor of Garvock, Mr William Wellwood, in despair at the ruin of his beautiful woods, went to stay at Pitliver, a mansion situated some three or four miles to the south-west of Dunfermline. Regarding Pitliver, it seems that Mr John Dempster, Advocate before the Court of Sessions, acquired the lands and barony of Pitliver about 1622 and later sold the estate to Mr Wellwood.

Many of these rebuilt houses displayed what were known as 'fire-stanes' usually consisting of suitable texts and the house-owner's initials. One of these can still be seen on the north side of east High Street on a house that was only partially destroyed. Another house was at the top of the Crosswynd and showed an elaborately-carved square stone on which was inscribed 'Seeing that in so brief a space, on the 25th May 1624 so much desolation was caused by a fire and the fury of the flaming blast, then O consider the dreadful blazing pyres which the breath of Jehovah, as if with a torrent of brimstone, will for ever keep in flames.' The initials, M.R.D. probably referred to Master Robert Drury. Other stones were removed during alterations, from the west wall of this house. One displayed the announcement in Latin 'M.W.D. built this house from the foundations'. These stones may now be seen at the west end of the nave in the Abbey.

The opportunity afforded by this disastrous event was not lost. Many of the re-built houses were of a larger and better design though in the main streets wooden fronts still projected above the first stone storey, outside stairs encroached on the roadway and only the HieGate was causewayed. Apparently the Market Cross suffered no damage, which was fortunate, as a new and more elegant structure had replaced the old one which had been erected there in the twelfth century. The new cross stood at the foot of Crosswynd, consisting of a small octagonal building from which rose the Pillar-stone, supporting a unicorn. There was also a stone pavement, reached from the inside by a few steps, from which, over a low parapet, the town's officer read public announcements. The Provost and magistrates themselves ascended these steps and proclaimed the name of a new Monarch and drank the Royal toast on the occasion of a Royal birthday. The cross stood there till 1752 when more will be said about its future fate.

In 1635, eleven years after the fire, the number of people living in the town and suburbs, according to a census taken at that time was about 1850.

Dunfermline High Street 1920s

9
Battle of Inverkeithing

Three years later, in 1638, the National Covenant was signed in Dunfermline. This document, drawn up by Alexander Henderson and Johnstone of Warriston, consisted of a very large sheet of vellum parchment and carried an imposing array of signatures — the Earl of Dunfermline, Sir Robert Halkett of Pitfirrane, James Durie of Craigluscar, Henry Wardlaw of Pitreavie, William Wardlaw of Balmule, John Stanehouse and Mr Samuel Row, assistant ministers in the Kirk of Dunfermline, with some two hundred other names. The opening lines of the Confession of Faith referred to its first appearance when the King and his household subscribed their names to it, with further additions in 1581 when ordained again by the Lords of Privy Council and Acts of General Assemblies and again in 1590 with a strong insistence on 'the maintainance of the true religion and the King's person.'

This document was first in the possession of the Earl of Dunfermline or his factor, William Walker, Provost of the town. His descendant, another William Walker of Rhodes, Clerk of the Regality, handed it over to the Rev. Ralph Erskine, soon after to become junior minister of the parish who seems to have presented it to the session of his newly formed Secession Church, Queen Anne Street, about 1740. After his death Mr Erskine's son gave it to the Rev. Mr Fisher of Glasgow who bequeathed it again to the Queen Anne Street congregation in whose possession it still remains.

In 1643, seven years after the National Covenant, the

Solemn League and Covenant for the reformation and defence of the true religion was read by Mr Robert Kay to a congregation in the Abbey church 'so that none could be found to plead ignorance thereof but that they may be prepared to sweare to it and subscribe the next Lord's Day.' This document was open for signatures on four dates in November. It is printed and contained in a quarto-sized book, having on the outside board 'for the Kirk of Dunfermling'. Apparently on the third of March, 1644, forty-six pence was paid for binding the Covenant and giving it a new cover. This interesting document is also in the possession of the Session of Queen Anne Street — now Erskine Church.

The Solemn League and Covenant was essentially a mutual bond entered into between Scotland and England for the better protection of the Protestant religion, the prevention of the spread of Papacy and Prelacy and the preservation of the liberties of the kingdom in peace and unity. It would seem that the Protestant religion was at that time in a state of some confusion as, for some months before the Covenant was presented for signatures, the same worthy citizens of Dunfermline had witnessed, no doubt with satisfaction and approval, the burning of four witches at the witch-loan while two others died in prison. Witch-watchers had been appointed to seize and put in ward all reputed witches and so six unfortunate old woman — Grissel Morris, Margaret Brand, Katharine Elder, Agnes Kirk, Margaret Donaldson and Isobel Millar — were put on trial, the judgment being a foregone conclusion. Four of them were taken by cart to the witches' dub near the gallows by the road to Townhill and there placed in the middle of a 'pile of wood with their hands and feet tied. The pile was then set on fire. At the loan there was a muddy pool known as the witches' dub into which a woman suspected of witchcraft might be thrown. If she sank she was innocent but nevertheless dead by drowning. If she floated, buoyed up perhaps, by her voluminous clothing, she was obviously a witch and, taken from the dub, was given to the flames. Of the two women who died in prison one was Janet Fenton. Her body was 'carted to the witch-knowe and cast into a hole without a coffin'. The other, Isobel Marr, managed to hang herself while in prison; she was also carted to the witch-knowe and buried there. The person who probably officiated on these grim occasions was Patrick Mayne, the local hangman.

No doubt the citizens of the town who believed so firmly in the devil and all his works were greatly disturbed and frightened by these uncanny happenings and before they had had time to recover the town was struck by an even more fearful enemy — the plague.

The Kirk Session Records report that on 19th October 1645 meetings 'were not frequent because of the pestilence that was then in the parish and increased in the same so that many died.' On the 25th November, things were getting worse. 'Because the number of the poor did increase in this tyme of plague many tradesmen put to penurie for want of commercing and handling of geir and money which was then dangerous to use and little alms colectit; therefore it was thot fit that meill should be given to the poor for their present help.' Plague-stones or dishes where money could be washed in water were placed at all the ports of the town. Dr Henderson refers to two that, built into the wall, were once to be seen in the Tron Close on the north side of the High Street. Another precaution taken was the fumigating of bed-clothes and wearing apparel in a closed apartment 'full of peat-reek.'

Dunfermline must have been a grim place with people falling dead in the streets or crawling away to die in a corner, with the dead-carts rolling over the cobbles in the dark watches of the night and the walls echoing to the sound of harsh voices calling 'Bring out your dead.' There were those who fled from the town in the hope of escaping the fatal infection but they could only expect a hostile reception when they sought new lodgings and no doubt many fell by the wayside. In the old pre-Reformation days monks and nuns might have been there to help the sick and dying, but now some of the old spitals were empty or destroyed and only a few Good Samaritans came forward to help their stricken friends and neighbours. Voluntary contributions were collected by various parish ministers and elders which went some way to relieving the distress of those who were not able to pay for burials. Corn was also distributed free and rough timber houses erected on the town-muir to accommodate those 'whose condition seemed desperate.'

No-one knows the real toll caused by this pestilent visitation but time passed and things improved again. Life went on and it was not long before the Kirk Session was once more exerting its authority.

On the fifth of March, 1648, an unfortunate old woman, charged with common scolding and drunkenness, was condemned to stand with the branks in her mouth on a market-day for two hours before noon, while in October, of the same year, another woman for much the same offence was carted and scourged through the town, marked with a hot iron and banished from the parish. The sentence was carried out by the magistrates.

In addition to all this the worthy citizens had the excitement of seeing a real warlock burned at the Witches' Knowe. After being 'straitlie posed and dealt with by the ministers and the watchers' he confessed that he had made a pact with the devil to be his servant for twenty-four years, and so his fate was sealed.

It seems that these witch-watchers followed a curious profession. There is an entry in the Dunfermline Kirk Session records regarding payment of some of them — 'to four watchers of the witch Margaret Macdonald for five days and five nichts, two of thame being on the watch at their severall terms to ilk of them for ilk day and ilk nicht six pounds Scots.'

In those days when communications between towns were difficult, when there were no proper roads and floods or snow could isolate a community for weeks no doubt the citizens of Dunfermline, absorbed with their own problems of survival with plague and death and supernatural enemies hovering over them, had little thought to spare for what was going on in the world outside their parish boundaries and little knowledge of how England had drifted into civil war. It was all so far away and of little concern except, perhaps, for the younger men of the town who crossed the border with the Covenanting army. At home the ministers in their pulpits raged against the King's perfidy and sinister intention towards the Reformed Church.

For three years twenty thousand Scots remained on English territory at their host's expense, intent upon saving England's soul by the establishment of the Presbyterian Church government. Later, when Cromwell's Model Army defeated the Royalists at Naseby, Scottish help was no longer needed and the Covenanters returned to their own country to face the threat offered by successes of Montrose, Lieutenant-General of the King till his power was broken at the battle of Philiphaugh. It would be with mixed feelings that Dunfermline townsfolk heard of the King's subsequent surrender to the Scottish army near Newark and of his delivery to the English Parliamentary forces with the stipulation that no harm should come to his person. This stipulation was later ignored when the King was put on trial for his life and condemned to death. The news of his execution in January 1649 would come as a great shock and sorrow to the whole of Scotland and Dunfermline was probably specially afflicted by the thought of the heads-man's axe. Many in the town could remember Charles as the little boy who rode his pony through the woods and charmed them all with his shy smile, his halting speech. There was the Palace where he had played with his brothers and sisters. There was the window of the room where, forty-nine years ago, he had been born.

The Scottish Estates lost no time in proclaiming Charles II King of England, Scotland, France and Ireland. This greatly offended the English 'Rump' Parliament which abolished the monarchy and proclaimed that anyone recognising Charles II as King would be guilty of treason. The Scottish Commissioners, sent to Breda to treat with Charles, found that, though he was ready to accept the crown, he strongly objected to some of the conditions which went with it. Months of argument and hesitation followed and it was not until 1650 that Charles came to Scotland, escorted by a Dutch fleet and landing at St Andrews. Charles' subsequent visits to Dunfermline have been dealt

with in Chapter Six. He was crowned at Scone on New
Year's Day, 1651. Once again he was required to sign the
covenant and to listen to six sermons in one day.

Perhaps the first connection Dunfermline had with the
Civil War now afflicting both England and Scotland was
the installation of sixteen cannon on Inchgarvie, an islet in
the middle of the Firth of Forth, and the appointment of Sir
James Halkett of Pitfirrane as Captain of the small but
determined garrison. Shortly after his coronation at Scone,
Charles as the commander-in-chief of his army, visited
Inchgarvie to inspect the fortifications and there, in a
spirited address to the garrison, repeated his determination
to uphold the Covenant and if need be, die in its defence.

'I am confident,' he said, 'that none present shall distrust
me, as I have as much at stake as any of them, forbye the
oath to God to which I have bound myself as your King —
your Covenanted King.'

Whether or not the men believed him, they gave a good
account of themselves when, in the summer, Cromwell's
advance-guard rode out of Edinburgh to attempt the
crossing of the Forth. They had to make a detour to avoid
the fire of Sir James' cannon and landed near Limekilns;
marching eastwards under cover of night, they succeeded
in surprising the garrison of North Queensferry, most of
whom were taken prisoner. This made the main body's
crossing of the Forth much simpler and all day on Saturday
Major Lambert was busy ferrying over some two thousand,
five hundred of his men in sixty double shallops.

There seems to be some doubt about Inchgarvie's
ultimate fate. According to the Ordinance Gazetteer of
Scotland the command of the garrison was held by Captain
Roy of Aldivalloch. On the approach of about three
hundred men in boats when he had only twenty men left,
he spiked the guns, blew up the magazine and escaped to
the Fife shore. But in one of Cromwell's letters, dated 26th
July, 1651, he refers to 'the castle of Inchgarvie which lies
in the river almost in the middle between the North and
South Ferry called Queensferry, and was delivered into our
hands. They marched away with their swords and baggage,

leaving only their sixteen cannon and their arms and ammunition.'

While it may be difficult to see how a garrison could 'march away' from an islet only five furlongs in circumference, Inchgarvie achieved further fame over two hundred years later by forming the central support for the two great spans that make up the Forth Railway Bridge.

Of the subsequent skirmishings between the Royalists and the Parliamentary forces on that weekend in 1651, the citizens of Dunfermline would know little. The sudden influx of men and horses brought an unwonted bustle to the narrow streets which once again echoed to the clatter of military boots and weapons, while foreign tongues were heard in the merchants' booths, the town's alehouses. Charles' army was a motley one with French and Dutch mingling with men from the Border and kilted Gaelic-speaking chiefs with their trains of bearded clansmen. On hearing that Cromwell's army was across the Forth, the Royalist army marched south on the Sunday morning to man the Ferry Hills that sloped eastwards towards Inverkeithing, their cannon commanding the flatter land across which the English troops must advance.

Reports of what followed are confused but it seems that when a Scots force under General Holborn moved down Castland Hill to outflank the main body of the English, they were attacked by a well-posted company left there by General Lambert to combat this move. For a time the struggle was fierce and bloody, with the issue always in doubt, till, before a new charge of the English, General Holborn turned and fled down the northern slopes, carrying with him most of his own followers and some waiting in reserve. This retreat turned into a headlong flight towards the valley of the Pinkerton Burn, while the main attack by Lambert charged and scattered the left and centre of the Royalists. Not far from the Castle of Pitreavie Sir Hector Maclean of Duart and what remained of his five hundred clansmen met the fugitives and attempted to turn the tide of battle. But the sabres of the cavalry were too strong for them and nearly all of them perished by the walls of the castle.

When it was all over and the survivors of Charles' defeated army had fled towards the west, taking him with them, the women of Dunfermline came down to look for their sons and husbands, brothers and fathers among the corpses that lay piled on the field of battle 'like stooks at hairst', and all through the long July night the search went on, while sad little processions escorting a rude bier or a wounded man, wound their slow way back to town. History does not relate what happened to the bodies of those dead men who were not claimed by relatives but, almost two hundred years later, in February, 1851, some labourers, digging a trench in the battlefield, uncovered a large number of human bones and a leather bag filled with coins of the Charles II period.

After the battle, the victorious army, led by Lambert and Overton, made its way to Dunfermline, where they behaved with a good deal of brutality, wrecking St. Leonard's chapel and the chapel of St. Mary in the Nethertown. The Kirk sessions records report that on various occasions Cromwell's men were guilty of breaking into the church and stealing the collection-money.

Charles, of course, had made his escape and with a large force of Scottish troops he went south to England to raise another army which was defeated by Cromwell at the battle of Worcester. After that the king without a country went to the Continent where he waited in poverty and impatience for a chance to reclaim his inheritance.

English soldiers seem to have been stationed in Dunfermline for some considerable time as various references are made to them in the Burgh and Kirk Sessions records for several years after the battle of Inverkeithing. Some of the natives evidently fraternised with them for, at different times, William M'Kay, Christine Thomson of the New Row and Bessie Kinsman were sharply rebuked and admonished 'for putting the stone in time of service with the English soldiers in the Kirkyard' and for selling drink and barrels of ale to the English. In 1655 the Provost had to protest to the captain, asking him to restrain his soldiers from drinking in brewers' houses on the Sabbath in time of sermon and the captain sent some of his sergeants through the town with orders to that effect. As late as 1656 the Palace and Queen's House were occupied by Cromwell's troops, described as a vile, lawless, rough set.

It remains to end this chapter with a footnote. Mr. Robert Kay, minister of the first charge of Dunfermline parish church, was bold enough to pray for King Charles the Second and for this he was imprisoned on Inchgarvie by Cromwell's soldiers. This detention did not last long as, through the efforts of commissioners sent by the Kirk Session of Dunfermline to the Commander in Chief, he was released and allowed to return to his work in Dunfermline. He must have found the islet an eerie dwelling-place with the wind screaming round the ruined walls like the voices of those drowning and dying men-at-arms.

The Little Dam — corner of Carnegie Street and Damside Street

10
Covenanters

The restoration of Charles the Second in the year 1660 seems to have gone unremarked in Dunfermline but a year later Burgess Peter Walker, was appointed one of the collectors of the King's annuity of forty thousand pounds sterling. In the same year came the news to the town of the death of Elizabeth, once Queen of Bohemia, eldest daughter of James VI. She had, like Charles, been born in the Palace but as that had been sixty-five years ago it would be unlikely that anyone would remember her, a gay, beautiful princess with all the fatal charm of the Stuarts.

As it was, the citizens of the town were concerned with more mundane immediate matters, such as the repairs to the Kirk and the draining of the Kirkyard which was frequently flooded at rainy seasons. Timber and slates were brought from Limekilns and James Henderson and David Turnbull, glazing wrights, were employed to mend the roof of the Kirk with cakes of lead while voluntary contributions were collected by deacons and elders from everyone in the parish to pay for work done in the Kirkyard. It seems that east of the friars' yard between the top of St Margaret Street and the New Row, the monks had constructed a small fish-pond to supply themselves with fish, and a burn, running westwards from this pond, went out at the west end of the churchyard, passed under St Catharine's Wynd and ultimately joined the Tower burn, The work done was evidently satisfactory. Adam Anderson reported to the Sessions regarding the way the money collected amounting to £156 had been spent on 'drying the kirkyairds' and the Session approved his accounts.

In 1662 the name of Mr. Robert Kay, minister of the first charge appears again, this time in a supplication from 'some gentlemen of the parish' that he was not strong enough for 'so great a charge' and that the Bishop should replace him. Kay demitted office in 1665 and became curate in the parish of Stowe. In the following year the Kirk records announced that the King's birthday and restoration would be celebrated on Friday, 29th May. This celebration of the Royal Birthday became an annual event till the death of George III in 1820.

This was a time of great and significant changes in matters concerning the religion of the whole country. Episcopacy had been restored by the Presbyterians, and the adherants of the Covenant now suffered the persecution that they had meted out to those who had disagreed with them. The Solemn League and Covenant was burned in London in 1661 and again in Linlithgow on the King's birthday in 1662. Parish ministers were expected to accept their charge from recently appointed bishops and when they refused they lost their positions. In Scotland Archbishop Sharp, sometime minister of Crail, was particularly severe against Non-conformist ministers; country people, meeting for worship in private houses or farm-steadings, were driven out to gather in the folds of the hills and there to be harassed by merciless men like Dalziel and Claverhouse.

In June, 1670, the first armed conventicle was held on the Hill of Beath, some four miles north-west of Dunfermline, when the preacher, the celebrated Mr. John Blackadder who had been ejected from his parish of Troqueer, spoke to about two thousand people. A small force of militia, intent on dispersing the congregation, was met by armed men on watch and was persuaded to retire without actually coming to blows. On news of this reaching Archbishop Sharp in Edinburgh he was **greatly displeased** and instituted proceedings against some of the many landed gentlemen who had attended the conventicle.

Robert Wellwood of Touch, near Dunfermline, was one who confessed to the Council that he had been present; he was fined five hundred marks and imprisoned till it was

paid, together with a bond of two thousand marks ensuring
that he would not frequent any other meetings. In spite of
fines and imprisonment, however, conventicles were still
held, usually on the Hill of Beath, and in 1677 Sir
Alexander Bruce of Broomhall was fined £1200 (Scots) for
not making his servants sign the Bond of Conformity and
abstaining from attending conventicles.

After the barbarous murder of Archbishop Sharp on
Magnus Moor in Fife in May 1679 the persecution of the
Covenanters became even more severe and Fife was
harshly dealt with, perhaps because the intrepid preacher,
Richard Cameron, was from Falkland. He headed a sect
that bore his name and was killed with a large number of
his followers by Bruce of Earlshall's troopers at the battle of
Airdmoss. In Dunfermline there were frequent searches of
private houses where it was reported religious meetings had
been held and those who would not accept the Episcopalian
system of government continued to be severely punished by
fines and imprisonment. Another Wellwood, James, was
arrested on suspicion of correspondence with some fugitives
in Holland and appeared before the Sheriff at Cupar.

The accession of James after the death of his brother
King Charles brought further persecution for he refused to
take the oath that bound the Kings of Scotland to defend
the Protestant religion and soon the government of the
country was in the hands of the Catholics. There was great
unrest everywhere until there came the Glorious Revolution in 1688 and the scene was changed. James the Seventh
was gone and his daughter Mary with William her
husband had taken his place. Mr John Gray was appointed
the first Presbyterian minister in Dunfermline and a year
later, due to his infirmity, the first Presbytery was held in
the town at the Meeting House, instead of at Kirkcaldy.
There is some doubt as to where this Meeting House was
held, whether in the Queen's House or in the large hall of
the Marquis of Tweeddale's house on the west side of the
Kirkgait and indeed the whole situation seems confused.
Mr Graham, who had not taken the Oath of Submission to
the Presbytery, was nevertheless allowed to remain in
possession of his benefice and to officiate in the parish-

church on one half of the Sabbath while the Presbyterians had Mr John Gray as their own minister. During the later incumbency of Mr Kemp from 1701-1715, the Presbyterian congregation met for worship in the parish-church on one half of the Sabbath while the Episcopalians held their services in the Meeting House and occupied the church for the afternoon services alternately. This arrangement continued till Mr Graham was finally deposed from his office as Episcopalian minister of the first charge of Dunfermline church in June 1701.

At this time there was a good deal of trouble over the taking of another oath, this time one of allegiance to King William and Queen Mary, an Oath that ended 'I shall defend Their Majesties' title and government against the late King James and his adherents and will try enemies who either by secret or open attempts shall disturb or exercise Their Majesties in the possession of same.'

Mr Thomas Marshall, minister of Carnock in 1679, who appears to have been a man of forthright opinions, was deposed for not reading from the pulpit the Proclamation Act and for not praying for William and Mary, 'instead praying that he hoped to see King James on his throne before Lammas.'

In the same year, 1689, the minister of the first charge of Dunfermline parish-church, Mr Thomas Graham and Mr Simon Coupar also got into trouble over not reading the Act. Both declared they were not guilty and were acquitted.

Five years later the Dunfermline Burgh records have a note saying that John Cowier, tresurer, was authorised to pay Laurence Henderson twenty-three marks for mending and gilding the King's Arms which hung in the council-chamber of the Tolbooth. No mention is made of the Queen's name but a few months later the town-councillors, led by the Provost, Sir Charles Halkett of Pitfirrane, were taking the oath of allegiance to Their Majesties, King William and Qreen Mary 'engaging to defend their Royal title and government against the late King James and his adherents.'

Sir Charles Halkett had received two Royal patents from Charles the Second, first a baronetship in Nova Scotia,

25th January, 1662 and a second on 25th January, 1671. As Burgess of Dunfermline Sir Charles had been a member of the Committee of Convention formed by the Scottish Parliament at the Revolution and in 1689 was appointed one of the Commissioners to treat with England on the matter of the Union. In 1679 he was elected Provost of Dunfermline, thus beginning a long connection with the town, his annual re-election to the office being brought to a close by his sudden death in 1697. As Sir Charles had died only a fortnight or so after his re-election as Provost he was accorded the honour of a public funeral and various officials had to busy themselves with unfamiliar arrangements.

A number of townscrafts, nominated by the deacon-conveners, and common burgesses, nominated by one baillie, mounted on horseback, were to accompany the Magistrates to Pitfirrane while those on foot awaited the cortège at the Port. This was the East Port for apparently the West Port in St Catharine's Wynd was too narrow for a hearse to pass through. So the funeral processions, escorted by many of the local gentry as well as the Town Council, came from Pitfirrane along the low south road to the Nethertown, up the New Row, through the East Port with its wide archway, down the High Street and the Kirkgait into the churchyard. In the parish-church, so greatly shorn of its former splendour, the minister and the family vault waited to receive the illustrious dead.

In those days funerals were carried out with much ceremony and even the poorest families managed to hire a mortcloth and pay the gravedigger's fee. The mortcloths, one of velvet and one of cloth, were hired out by the Mortcloth Society of Dunfermline, a purely civilian or lay organisation which had nothing to do with the church. The town was divided into districts with a member as manager of each district, with half of these members being elected annually. Cloths were regularly examined, the treasurer kept an exact account of income and expenditure and a balance, when exceeding one pound sterling, was deposited in the Savings Bank. Members, when requiring a cloth, had to present their certificate to the manager of their district who gave them an order authorising the officer to attend on the appointed day.

The mortcloth was used to cover the coffin at the kisting. This was an important ceremony with the body in its coffin being placed in a room of the bereaved family. Neighbours, the minister and maybe an elder were present to offer up suitable prayers. The lid of the coffin was not screwed down till the time came for taking the body to the graveyard. In 1686 an Act of Parliament was passed, called the Act for burying in Scots linen when 'it was ordained that no person whatsoever of high or low degree should be buried in any old shirt, sheet or shroud except in plain linen made and spun in the Kingdom and without lace or point Hollands or other linens, foreign-made, or silk, hair, woollen, gold or silver or any other stuff under the penalty of 300 pounds Scots for a nobleman or 200 pounds Scots for any other person for each offence.'

One half of the penalty was to go to the informer and the other half to the poor of the parish where the body was interred. For the better detection of evasions of this Act every minister had to keep a register of all persons buried in his parish and to him was handed a declaration by the family that the dead person had been prepared for burial in the manner prescribed by the Act. It was also required that no wooden coffin should exceed one hundred marks Scots in value for persons of the highest quality and so proportioned for others of lower rank under a penalty of two hundred marks Scots for each offence.' As might have been expected this Act was evaded by every possible means so that, within nine years, in 1695 it was found necessary to renew and ratify afresh the provisions and penalties of the Act, with the addition that, under a fine of forty marks, seamstresses were forbidden to make or sew a shroud, sheet or shirt of any other material than that allowed by the act.

Up till the end of the eighteenth century those who committed suicide in Scotland were not only denied the use of the mortcloth but all the rites of christian burial. Coffinless and unmourned the remains were conveyed at midnight to the march boundary of two parishes and deposited in neutral ground with a stake driven through the body, thus fixing it to the earth and denying it all hopes of a resurrection. The body was considered vile and the earth where it lay polluted; the coarse wooden framework on which it was dragged along was afterwards burnt to ashes. Later on the suicide was allowed the use of a coffin but the rest of the grisly ritual remained unaltered for many years.

About this time it is cheering to note that various acts of charity can be recorded. A House of Correction for idle beggars and vagabonds was to be built while a collection was made for the benefit of poor scholars and teachers whose names appeared on a roll made for that purpose. In 1675 money was contributed for the ransom of two captives with the Turks, Walter Gibbison and John Reid, men of Inverkeithing. In the same years Sir Henry Wardlaw of Pitreavie, founded a Hospital at Masterton, a nearby village, to house 'four widows, women of honest fame, relicts of honest men who lived on the lands of Pitreavie belonging to him and his successors.'

According to Fernie's history each woman was to have a room and six bolls of meal yearly, or six bolls of oats and three bolls of bere at the option of the patron. Another legacy to the poor was made by John Drysdale of the Nethertoun who left to the burgh of Dunfermline five hundred merks, the income from which was to be paid to the Kirk Session and laid out for the maintenance of poor scholars at school. A year later the Kirk Session mortified into the hands of Dunfermline Town Council the sum of £1000 merks Scots — or £55-11-1½ — for the use of the Doctor of the Grammar School. The Session and the Town Council shared the right to appoint the Doctor.

On the 13th July 1678 Patrick Mudie appeared before the Kirk Session to request permission to set up a school at the Gellets for the children of that district who lived too far from the town to attend the town schools. Permission was granted and he was licensed to teach these children providing always 'that he live orderly and regularly as became one in such a station.'

This might be the place to say something about the Court of Regality and its long and complicated history. It is understood to have been created by the early charters of the

Abbey and was probably as old as the Abbey itself. It enjoyed complete independence and power over those living within the bounds of the Abbot's Burgh and the King was unable to interfere except in the case of treason. Thus, as the lands and possessions of the Abbey increased so did the influence of those in charge of the Court of Regality. Accused people, handed over to its justice, had to abide by its sentence and the Court dealt not only with petty thefts but with arson, rape, murder and robbery. The more common crimes such as breaches of the peace with involved stories of family feuds were usually punished by fines.

Robert the Bruce granted to the Court a coquet or seal which certified that the goods thus marked had paid the customs due on them and it was at this time that Dunfermline was first known as an Abbot's Burgh, as opposed to the settlement which had been a King's Burgh in the twelfth century.

In course of time as their affairs increased, the officers of the Court of Regality consisted of a Steward, Bailies and a Sergeant who carried out the main duties of the Court such as making arrests and calling the suits to court. He carried a wand as his sign of office and when he displayed it broken to the Court this was a sign that he had met with resistance in the execution of his duties and that the authority of the Court had been defied. There was also a scribe or clerk who was probably a notary and made all the official records. A Dempster and a Chamberlain collected the Abbot's rents which came not only from the burgh but also from lands and buildings, churches and tithes. The amount of money thus collected was very considerable and made Dunfermline Abbey one of the wealthiest in the country but the end of the Court of Regality came with the end of the Abbey's authority in the chaos of the Reformation. After this there were no Regality records till they began again in 1582. By this time its functions were not ecclesiastical nor commercial for in 1587 Hew Watt, a vagabond, was tried by the Regality Court of Dunfermline and found guilty of stealing cattle. Hew must have stolen the cattle from the Laird of Baldridgeburn for he was hanged on 'Baldie's' private gallows.

This is a very condensed account of what was a most important part of the town's history but there is not enough space here to go into these matters in more detail.

It is probable that meetings of the Court after 1621 were held in a large house on the north side of East Nethertoun with this date over the door. It was a building of two stories with only one window on the street, the lower floor having a solidly vaulted ceiling while the floor of the upper flat was composed of solid masonry in lime and ashlar. There were two strongly-made front doors in the entrance and the staircase was built in the thickness of the walls, leading up to the Council chamber. Here there was an enormous fire-place and the grate was a very elaborate one which was bought by Sir Joseph Paton when the building was demolished in 1862. The lower flat was the black hole or prison. The Court must have seen a lot of local history made as, in 1780, when the garret of the house was explored, over forty volumes of its records were found.

These records would have been concerned with many interesting and illuminating events in local history for the offices held by the Roman Catholic church passed, after the Reformation into the hands of those noblemen who had received much of the confiscated Church property. Before Robert Pitcairn, Secretary of State to James VI died, he and the convent of Dunfermline in 1580 created the office of heritable Bailie of the Regality and conferred it upon David Durie, probably the nephew of George Dury, former Abbot. The charter conferred on him and his successors mails of money, all the feu-farms victuals and other duties formerly payable to the monastery from all lands belonging to it on the northern side of the Forth. It also declared that the foresaid Bailie and his successors in office should have free entertainment in the monastery for themselves and twelve followers, horse and foot, in meat and drink and suitable lodgings and accommodation whilst they should happen to be detained at the three-yearly head-courts and other courts of the Regality for the administration of justice. In 1596 David Drury, the first Bailie, resigned his offices and all its perquisites into the hands of Queen Anne, as Lady of Dunfermline, in favour of Alexander Seton,

President of the Court of Session by the title of Lord Urquhart, later Earl of Dunfermline who was reconfirmed in these privileges and office, adding in 1641 a crown lease for nineteen years of the feu-duties and teinds of the whole lordship and regality of the town. This crown lease was renewed at intervals by the Tweedales who had inherited it, all through the centuries and the different reigns that followed till 1780 when the application was refused and the new lease granted to the Countess of Rothes, the Earl of Elgin and others which continued till March 1838 when the feus and teind duties became payable to the Crown under the management of the Commissioner of Woods and Forests.

Besides the office of Bailie of the Regality there was also that of the Constable or Keeper of the Palace, with adjoining yards and pends, this office being maintained by the teinds of Masterton and Pitliver. Queen Anne, by charter, conferred this appointment in 1586 also on the Earl of Dunfermline and his heirs for ever, an appointment which we have seen was of short duration.

Another heritable office was that of Sergeant or Provost, head-officer of the Regality. The first commission was granted to John Wellwood of Touch, whose family had for generations been head-mayors or officers of the Abbey. The fee for this office was a certain quantity of oatmeal from the west mill of Kirkcaldy, called Sergeant's corn, with forty shillings Scots, payable out of the lands of Touch.

It would seem that the town, at this time, was hardly prospering. In 1694, for the first time, the burgh records mention the burgh debt amounting to 5573 merks (£309-12- sterling) and three years later the Burgh Treasurer 'because he was straitened for money to do ye toun's affaires' was allowed to borrow 600 merks from Thomas Adie. Private persons also seemed to be in serious want. To William Reid, son of the late Provost the Treasurer was ordered to donate six lippies of meal and seven pence weekly for his maintenance from May 1697 to the first of September 1698 as he was 'almost starving at that time,' while Helen Watson received a charitable gift to buy medicaments for her daughter who is sick of ye passion.'

After a severe winter when snow lay from January till the beginning of April, the town was also faced with a dearth, due no doubt to the failure of successive harvests and the sickness of their cattle, and the town council had to come to the aid of families of poor people who were literally starving. Lists of householders who were in want but who had not applied for help were made out and the Bailies directed to allocate such charitable sums. There were badges for the poor to wear when they were allowed to beg on each Tuesday and Saturday; this helped the constables and town officers to see that strange beggars from other parts were sent out of the town.

At this time the town officials included treasurer, clerk, procurator fiscal, drummers, pipers and a man called Adam Steveson the younger to wind up and keep the town clock in order.

At the end of the seventeenth century the population of Scotland amounted to one million, one hundred thousand. In 1696 crops had been ruined by storms and droughts. Summers had been ruined by drenching rains and winters by frost and snow. Men were frequently to be seen carrying corpses along the roads, single-handed, to the cemetery and on these roads women and children were to be found dying of cold and hunger. Everywhere Kirk Session records are full of details about making poor folks' graves and paying the preacher for his services in the churchyard. During the scarcity the free importation of grain was allowed while every farmer was forced to thrash his grain and forbidden to sell any of it on the road back from the mill. Current prices were announced from the pulpit and as everyone was certain that all this misery was caused by God's rightful wrath, fast-days and days of constant prayer were held in the hope of improving the situation.

Agriculture was badly managed. The farmer was only interested in his infield, the part lying close to his house. All the manure was put on this infield, while portions of the outfield would be cropped by oats, sometimes for three successive years. Then, exhausted, it was allowed to lie fallow for a year. There were few fences and no dykes or hedges. Cattle wandered everywhere unless they were herded. Ploughs were huge and unwieldy, drawn by four meagre oxen or a couple of horses like shelties. One man — the strongest — held the plough with its coulter and sock of iron, another drove the animals and cleaned 'the fur-board' while a third led the team walking backwards, and a fourth went in front with a spade to 'even the furs'. Half-an-acre a day was a fair day's work and a farmer could not yoke a plough till Candelmass. Oats were sown late, barley often not till May or June. Threshing was done by a flail and winnowed by the wind. The fanners invented by one Meikle in 1720 were refused. The wind was God's breath.

Rents were generally paid in kind and landlords had to keep big barns to contain their stores of poultry, oxen and sheep which provided liberally for their needs during the winter months. Rings were made to 'size' eggs. Large ones were twelve to the dozen, next fifteen to the dozen and the smallest eighteen to a dozen. On the great estates round Dunfermline grinding mills were found wherever there was sufficient water to provide the necessary power. Carts were of very rude construction, the wheels being of solid wood with a hole in the middle, and were not in general used till about 1760 when the roads were made. Even near Edinburgh, up to 1730, hay, straw and coal were transported on horseback.

Then in 1696 the whole country was stirred by the news of the Darien Scheme. In Dunfermline the town council, moved by the general excitement roused by Mr Paterson's eloquence, subscribed ten pounds towards the venture, shared the rejoicing when its success seemed assured and the national mourning when ruin and disaster followed. Some of the wealthier citizens of the town lost their money and many young men, who had sailed away from Leith or Glasgow in the hope of finding a new Eldorado, lost their lives. It took Scotland a long time to recover from what was indeed a national disaster.

Old Mill Port

11
Local Customs

The opening of the eighteenth century found the Town and Royal Burgh of Dunfermline in a bad way, with the magistrates and council appealing for aid from the Convention of Royal Burghs. This appeal specially referred to the malting which was carried out by no fewer than eight breweries, for the town at that time was renowned more for its ale than its linen, though one of the native weavers found fame by weaving a shirt on his loom.

On the twenty-first of March 1702 Anne was proclaimed Queen on the death of William the Third. There seems to have been little excitement in the town over this event, though the announcement was made in the usual style and town's piper and drummer received a shilling each for their attendance at the ceremony at the Cross.

Regarding church matters as explained in the previous chapter, the situation remained confused and it seems that when the Meeting House proved unsuitable, Lord Yester, later Lord Tweeddale was asked to give them the use of one of his vaults in the Abbey, a request which was granted. Also just to prove that there is nothing new under the sun, complaints were made by the education authorities against the existence of several Private Schools in the burgh.

Mr Patrick Dykes, Master of the Grammar School, sent a protest to the town council regarding John Anderson and Thomas Hanna who had opened their own schools in the town. The Council unanimously decided to forbid these gentlemen and any others with the same intention, unless their pupils were under seven years of age. If this decree were disobeyed they would be liable to a fine of twenty pounds (Scots) one half to go to the town, the other to the schoolmaster. The same trouble arose frequently in the years to come.

After the turn of the century various buildings in the town seemed to be suffering from neglect. In 1702 the East and Crosswynd Ports had to be restored as they were reported to be in a ruinous state, the Spittal Bridge was considered dangerous and was not rebuilt till the end of 1706, and in 1708 the north gable and part of the front wall of the Palace fell, along with part of the roof, creating a mound of debris that covered all the west slope of the ground.

In spite of the expense thus incurred the magistrates and town councillors made a generous gift to Sir James Halkett who, in addition to his family's past efforts in connection with the town, had presented a foot mantle for the Provost to wear at the riding of Parliament. This gift consisted of discharging various annual rents paid by him to the town, both past and present. They also ordered a 'press' to be made in which to keep the foot mantle. The fiscal received payment for keeping the mantle with half-a-crown added for keeping the casket in the kirk-seat.

Sad to relate, the Provost, Sir James Halkett of Pitfirrane, died as a result of a fall from his horse only a few months later. As the baronetcy thus became extinct, he was succeeded by his eldest sister Janet, married to Sir Peter Wedderburn of Gosford, who then assumed the arms and name of the Pitfirrane family. The following year Sir Peter seems to have got into trouble. The magistrates and council of the town were bitterly opposed to the Union of Parliaments between England and Scotland and they commissioned Sir Peter, who was their Parliamentary representative to 'vote and protest against the Union.' They received an assurance from Sir Peter that he would do as requested but when the time came he presented the address from the town council and voted for the Union. This inconsistency roused a great deal of criticism and ill-will against him but he must have had a winning way for he was elected Provost of the town for the next twenty-seven years.

The Union question had long been a vexed one in the country and the general opinion was that a great deal of corruption and bribery went on behind the scenes. In Scotland thirty-three burghs voted for the Union and twenty-nine against it. No doubt it is a coincidence that the privilege held by the Halkett family to export coal abroad was renewed by the Queen and the Union Parliament in London, just before the Union became an established fact.

A year later the town council was concerned about the burgh's weights and measures and sent Baillie Wilson to Edinburgh to arrange the purchase of new English weights and measures. Also two brass jugs were bought for the burgh, stamped by the Edinburgh Dean of Guild's stamp. English standards also had to be met over an iron ell and yard, likewise marked with the Dean of Guild's stamp. This anglicisation of Scotland was in fulfilment of the terms of the Act of Union.

The main concern of the citizens, however, at this time was a great snow storm that went on for eight days. The burns were all frozen hard and the town was cut off from the outside world till the thaw came, some six weeks later, bringing a dangerous flood in its wake. After that, life returned to normal with a routine of fairs, butter-markets, riding the marches for burgesses with the fine of half-a-mark for non-attendance. Chapmen in the public markets had to be provided with stands furnished by the owners of the houses or 'lands' before which the booths were set up. For their recreation there were horse-races, when the town council provided from the rates a saddle, also a bonnet with ribbons and a pair of stockings for the winner of a foot-race, and for their spiritual consolation there was Ralph Erskine, installed in the second charge in the Abbey.

He had been born near Cornhill in Northumberland, the son of a deprived Scottish Presbyterian minister. He was a man of very dogmatic opinions, impatient of the way the law of patronage was exercised by the church authorities and when he seceded from his charge in the Abbey a large number of his parishioners followed him to the tent in which he preached before a more commodious meeting-place was erected for him in Queen Anne Street, now known as the Erskine Free Church. In 1714 he was married to Margaret Dewar, only daughter of John Dewar of Lassodie. They lived in a modest home on the south side of the High Street and he continued with his ministrations to the faithful till his sudden death from fever in 1752. His imposing tomb can be seen on the north-east side of the Abbey graveyard. Unfortunately age and weathering has made its inscription difficult to read. He was not only a great preacher but also a poet, a musician, a teller of lighthearted stories, and he should be remembered as a brave man, an eloquent preacher and a friend of the people.

A few years later some members seceded from the Ralph Erskine Church and joined with others from Cairneyhill to form a new congregation which came to be known as the Anti-burghers, meeting for worship at Gillanderston Toll. In 1789 the Anti-burghers of Dunfermline built a church in Chalmers Street and engaged a minister of their own.

But before all this happened the townsfolk of Dunfermline found themselves caught up once again in the country's history. Rumour had it, backed by official letters from various authorities in Edinburgh, that Queen Anne was very ill and consequently there was some considerable doubt as to who should succeed her. The country might have to choose between the man the Jacobites called James VIII or George, Elector of Hanover and Luneberg, son of Sophia, a grand-daughter of James VI and I. His mother and then himself had been recognised as heirs to the throne of Great Britain and Ireland by the Act of Settlement in 1701 and to that of Great Britain by the Union of 1707 but this arrangement was not universally popular and though the new King was duly proclaimed by the magistrates and town-council on the Tolbooth Stair, at the Cross and the East Port, there were many in the town ready to join in the threatened rebellion in favour of the Stewart.

The town council, indeed, was so alarmed by the local discontent that they ordered Baillie Wilson and William Stevenson to buy at once one hundred pound weight of powder and six hundred pound weight of lead. That these precautions were not unnecessary was proved some months later when a detachment of Jacobites, four score of horse and three of Highland foot, led by Gordon of Glenbuckie, entered the town. They stabled their horses among the ruined walls of the monastery and their officers took up their quarters in the Queen's House, the two Constabulary houses and others in the neighbourhood. The regiment of horse was under the command of Major Graham but, like all the other officers, he was too eager to arrange for his own accommodation and enjoy a meal with a bottle of wine, to bother about the strong force of cavalry, led by Colonel Cathcart, which was waiting outside the town. Colonel — afterwards Lord — Cathcart profited by information received and entered the town at five o'clock in the morning with two parties of his dragoons, mounted and on foot. The Jacobite officers taken by surprise, put up little resistance and while the Highland regiment in the Abbey policies was not disturbed, a number of them were taken prisoner and taken away to Stirling. As this seems to be fair sample of Mar's tactics it is small wonder that the '15 rebellion had such little success.

No doubt the Dunfermline citizens were excited by the sight and sound of the Highlanders, but relieved when they all clattered away back to Perth and glad that their own force of 'fencibles' had not been called upon to use the powder and shot lodged in the cellar at the south-east end of the Palace, afterwards to be known as the Magazine. The visit of the rebels had, however, caused the town some expense, probably in food and fodder, and for a time the Royalist troops were stationed there, so that, some months later, the bailies were writing to ask the authorities in Edinburgh for recompense.

But the forming of the Gardeners' Society at this time shows that the citizens had more pleasant matters on their minds. The Society was meant to improve gardening, support its members and collect money on seeds brought from abroad. The Bond of Union was headed by the Marquis of Tweeddale and the Earl of Moray, and though the Society began in a small way it was not long before it possessed lands of about twenty acres, which divided into three parks, lay to the north-east, within five minutes' walk from the Cross. They were afterwards exchanged for town lands to the west with the payment of another £120. Coal was worked in its immediate vicinity and people moved in to feu the land and build on it. Accordingly, in 1816 the Chancellor of the Society and others planned out the ground and set off between thirty and forty feus. There was plenty of good water in the ground and the village came to be known as Gardeners' Town. By this time many new ideas had been introduced to deal with old age pensions for members over sixty-five, widows' pensions, funeral allowances and special endowments. The list of members cut right across society from the Marquis of Tweeddale, Lord Jedburgh, Lord Cumberland, the Earl of Kellie, Sir James Bruce of Kinross, the Duke of Atholl, Sir Henry Wardlaw of Balmule, the Earl of Strathmore, Lords Elphinstone and Crawford, James Oswald of Dunnikier, Patrick Wright, wig-maker, Alexander Miller, tenant of the Heugh Mills, John Maxwell, card-maker, Mr Wardlaw, minister, John Symon, glazier, Dugald Gedd, goldsmith from Edinburgh and many others.

Another society of some importance was the Conveners' Court, the membership of which seemed to consist of eight Deacons of Craft and their late Deacons, together with two town councillors, treasurers and joint managers of the Common Stock belonging to the Deacon-Conveners' Court. The first mentioned Deacon-Convener in 1686 was Thomas Elder and other names followed steadily down the centuries till the records apparently ceased about 1835. The Courts held their meetings in various places, such as the Session-house of the Abbey, the Tolbooth, the town-clerk's house as well as the homes of various citizens — James Barrowman, flesher, in 1765, James Mercer in 1771, Thomas Anderson in 1740, Deacon Bentine in 1749 and William Stenhouse in 1770. Meetings seem to have been held at the strange hour of five or eight in the morning while a few took place at noon. Only members of the town council were eligible for membership and each freeman on his admission to any of the crafts paid a fee of varying amounts to a box-master or treasurer in name of the Conveners' Court. There were also considerable sums drawn from the members of other incorporations and from outside parties in the form of interest upon sums loaned to them by the Court. In 1747 the Conveners' Council was called upon to contribute to the 'cess paid by force to the rebels', that is the Jacobite army in 1745-6 as the town council had found it difficult to meet the demand which amounted to £35- 1/- sterling. After some argument the members of the Council agreed to give various sums ranging from ten shillings to £1-15 and in the end £5 was handed over to the Treasurer.

The Court had a table seat in the Abbey church and most of their activities centred on looking after the deserving poor, money also being paid out for the support of indigent Court members, their children or wives. There were also other disbursements — meetings, dinners, suppers, demonstrations which meant unfolding their 'colours', journeys and subscriptions. Some items were twelve shillings spent at the Deacons' dinner — £28-18/- paid to 'the poor', four shillings for 'putting out the colour' on the King's birthday, George II. £133-6-8 lent to the Incorporation of Baxters, 6/- on ale at the transaction. In September 1734 the Deacons spent £4-3/- on election-day, no doubt drinking the health of the candidates, James Smith got £1-16/- for a pair of shoes and three shillings was paid to put slates on a member's roof. The sum of eight shillings was paid to the Bellman for advertising the 'roup of Ferguson's laigh-hoose'. This official received a coat and shoes at intervals. In 1760 it was suddenly decided that there were to be no more dinners paid for by the Court out of the Court's public stock of income.

The lives of the citizens were still subject to strict regulations. Their weddings were proclaimed or 'cried' in church for three successive Sundays and on the following Wednesday the bride invited her friends to her mother's house, while the bridegroom did the same with his. On Thursday furniture was sent to the new house — a chest filled with bedclothes, sheets, blankets and another full of clothes, an aumry or large press with two divisions, a chest of drawers, a spinning-wheel and a girnel with a quantity of meal, butter, bread and cheese.

The wedding took place in the bride's home and after it a procession moved in couples to the new house, being well pelted with slippers, divots and rubbish as they progressed through the streets. On arrival the best man threw coppers to the crowd. There were free weddings when everything was paid for by the bride's parents, dinner weddings when only dinner was provided and penny weddings when everyone present paid a shilling towards the cost of the entertainment.

When, in due course, a child was born to the happy couple, it was tightly wrapped in swaddling clothes by the midwife, arms bound to the sides, while in the living-room, the pot was put on the fire and a pudding was made of flour, butter, bread, ale and sugar which was served to all the neighbours who were invited to share in the celebrations. Then the emptied pot was put on again, filled this time with ale, brandy and sugar with some bread added, and this beverage, known as the Het Pint, was handed round and served out till both men and women were pleasantly tipsy.

Baptism was a solemn affair. The baby was carried by a young woman to the church. She was accompanied by a group of friends who, armed with a plentiful supply of oatcakes and cheese, handed them out to anyone they met. The first one to receive this donation was of some importance as not only did his 'luck' attach itself to the child, but he was expected, though never asked, to give it something for luck. The return from the church was usually followed by a modest feast.

High Street, Dunfermline

12
Poets and Inns

In 1723 Daniel Defoe visited Dunfermline in the course of his travels, looking for material for his *Journey through Scotland* which was published the following year. He seemed to regard the town with rather a jaundiced eye for, according to him, everything was in a decayed state. He spoke of the Palace as being one of two courts — the upper contained the Royal apartments and in the lower were the stables for horses, hounds and hawks and the men who attended them. Much of the church and choir was still a heap of rubbish with the tombs of the Kings of Scotland lying in the open air, including the black alabaster tomb of St Margaret. Apparently a Noble Cloister had been turned into a tennis court. Defoe was wrong in his reference to Royal tombs, being deceived by some flat stones that lay in the choir, but he certainly did not exaggerate when he mentioned the magnificent view of the Forth as seen from gaping windows in the ancient refectory.

No doubt Mr Defoe had heard of the *Ballad of Hardicanute* which had been published a few years earlier and was supposed to be the work of Elizabeth Halkett who had married Henry Wardlaw of Pitreavie. He may even have called upon her on his way south, though the lady was at first reluctant to acknowledge the poem was hers. It was concerned with the battle of Largs fought in 1263 between Alexander of Scotland and Haco, King of Norway, and on the title page of the second edition it is stated that Hardicanute is a Fragment, being the First Canto of an Epic Poem with General Remarks and Notes.

Elizabeth Halkett outlived her husband, spending the years of her widowhood in a house at the head of the Crosswynd, on the north-east corner, and was buried in the Wardlaw vault on the south-eastern corner of the Abbey.

About this time it was decided by the town council that, in view of 'the robbing and stealing' which went on throughout the country, it would be as well to have a town-guard. The magistrates were therefore instructed to appoint a guard of ten men to keep watch every night in the mealmarket where they were to be supplied with coal and candles, under the command of a captain chosen by the magistrates. Not long after, the people who lived above the market complained to the town council about the noisy behaviour of these guards. Apparently a gun had gone off and 'the ball had gone up through the floor'. The Council dealt with this by ordering the guard-house to be plastered and some material lodged between the plaster and the floor.

Between the years 1717-1751 some six Acts of Parliament were passed, relating in great detail to all the processes and movements of every manufacturer and worker in the linen trade. Concerning flax, 'stamp-masters, riding-officers and surveyors' were directed to search for bad or 'damnified' flax-seed, report all offenders and examine all imported seed before it passed through the custom-house. Makers of spinning-wheels and measuring reels were obliged to stamp their names on every implement, while the flaxen or hempen yarn had to be made up for sale at home or for export in cuts, haers and hasps, and sold in spindles or parts of spindles. Dyes for the yarn had to be fast and those bleached by pigeons' dung or lime rejected. Any transgressor in these or other matters could be sent to prison, kept at hard labour or maybe publicly whipped. Every journeyman-weaver, setting up on his own as master-weaver, had to find security before a Justice of the Peace or a magistrate in the burgh and declare he would weave according to the law, remembering the instructions which included such details as running a coloured thread at the end of each piece, under the penalty of £5. Trademarks were also jealously guarded; there was a fine of £100 for counterfeiting another's. The theft of linen cloth or mixed linen fabrics or any thread or yarn to the value of ten shillings was, on conviction, punished by death or transportation for fourteen years. While linen cloth manufactured in Great Britain was exported duty-free, an Act of Parliament of 1748 prohibited the importation of French lawns and the wearing of such fabrics after March 1749. In the year 1753-54 linen cloth stamped in Scotland for sale amounted to nearly nine million yards and its value £406,816. It will therefore be seen from this that the Dunfermline linen industry was thriving and great ingenuity was shown in the invention of patterns such as 'The Weavers' Banner' which consisted of a large sheet of silk damask, with many different devices on each side. These framed the words on one side 'For the Weavers of Dunfermline 1734' and the weavers' motto Trust with Truth; on the other a St Andrew's Cross and the town's motto 'Nemo Me Impune Lacessit.' This flag was the work of James Blake and the weaving of different sides was considered to show great skill.

Other employments connected with the linen trade were warpers, lappers, winders and bleachers of yarn, designers or pattern-drawers, pattern-cutters and dyers. Women and girls worked as winders and pirn-fillers, yarn boilers and bleachers of cloth.

Perhaps the criticism of Defoe had had some effect for in 1728 the town council and heritors of the Abbey decided to repair part of the church, the steeple and the bells. Estimates were invited and the work was done at the cost of £647-1-10 Scots — about £34 sterling. The two bells, one large and one small, being cracked, were re-cast in Edinburgh and suitably inscribed with the dates and details of those responsible, and the weathercock was set on the steeple by David Wright. This, at least, would show the citizens how the wind was blowing.

It may be interesting to note at this point just what the main streets and buildings of the town looked like in the middle of the eighteenth century. The old Townhouse was then modest enough, a two-storied building facing up the High Street with a broad flight of steps leading to the upper

Dunfermline's first Townhouse

flat which was of wood and contained the dwelling and
office of the town clerk, with the debtors' room. The
ground floor was of stone and held the rooms of public
assembly, while the cellar was a prison. In front of the
Townhouse was the mill-lade or Tower burn which
supplied water to the neighbourhood. The burn was
enclosed by low dykes, with flat parapets which formed the
causeway and steps that permitted access to the water.
There was a pend formed by the Townhouse stair; the
burn passed through this, together with the causeway
which connected the Kirkgait to Collier Row. (Bruce
Street.) Almost opposite the nearby Tron well stood the
pillory which seems to have been a square pedestal placed
almost in the centre of the High Street, and from it
stretched a low flat wall which provided a counter for goods
brought for sale at the Townhouse. From the pillory to the
Market cross at the top of the High Street, the houses were
mostly of two storeys, the lower of stone, the upper of wood,
projecting over the street. A number of houses that had
once belonged to the court retainers and the clergy were all
of stone and Gothic architecture.

The Cross, standing in the middle of the street, was mounted on a pedestal highly ornamented with the town's arms and other national designs. These were removed to adorn the front of the next Townhouse and the pillar of the Cross became part of the building on the north side of the High Street. It now stands in a corner outside the Sheriff-court, shorn of all its former glory.

In the eighteenth century the site of the building now used as the Sheriff court was occupied by three very old thatched, two-storyed cottages. Later they were removed to make way for the Spire Inn. More wood and stone houses stretched on towards the East Port, where on the north side of the Port at the foot of Shaddo Wynd — now Bonnar Street — stood an ancient tenement, probably the mansion of some nobleman and opposite it, stretching out almost to the middle of the street was another old house to which was attached one side of the Old Port. Downhill to the south the New Row led down to Canmore Street. Between it and the High Street the whole area was occupied by gardens while from Canmore Street to Priory Lane, there was a large walled park, known as the Bleach — later Abbey Park Place. Here water from the town burn ran through various artificial channels. In the past the whole propery had belonged to the Abbey.

This road that plunged steeply downhill was from the earliest times known as the New Row. On the west side below Canmore Street a brewery had been established at the end of the seventeenth century and further down were substantial houses that later served a carter as stables. The date above one of the windows was 1695. Opposite what was to be Park Avenue there was a high retaining wall with buttresses and a square tower.

From the south a road came up through the Abbey Glebe to St Catharine's Wynd; there were no dwelling-houses here but various industries such as a nail-maker and a smithy. At that time the ruins of the Palace had no protecting wall and where trees later stood there was an unfenced kitchen garden.

There must have been many inns or taverns in Dunfermline at this time and this description of the Thorn Inn —

the thirteenth house from Moodie Street and the fifth from Reid Street — might apply to others though no doubt the thorn tree was unique. This was a fine old tree growing in front of the house and it was depicted on one side of a signboard which had on the other a man and a horse with the intimation 'British and Foreign Spirits, Dunfermline Ale and Porter. Entertainment for man and horse.'

The Thorn Inn was a building of two storeys with five small windows and an outside stair leading to the upper floor, which was let to tenants. Having pressed down the sneck and opened the door, the traveller entered the kitchen which was large and well furnished with a sanded floor and white-washed walls. On the back wall there was a long rack of shelves on each side of which hung cleeks, glittering flagons and stoups while the shelves were laden with pewter plates of varying sizes. There was a large fireplace and in winter a roaring fire gave the wet or windblown customer a warm welcome. Behind the kitchen was a snug little room with small windows looking out to the north. This was the parlour, the principal room of the house, with a large folding table, chairs and stools set in the centre. A cupboard filled one corner, its shelves crowded with crockery and a large china punch-bowl. On one side stood the landlady's oaken chest of drawers and on the other an old eight-day clock. Here there was another generous grate full of burning coal or logs; along the passage were two bedrooms. Unhappily the building fell into ruins about 1794 when it was taken down and replaced by a house built by a Mr William Brown of Kinross.

One would imagine that the Thorn Inn in its heyday enjoyed a reputation for good food and drink and cheerful hospitality. Not far away in Reid St. there was another inn which seems to have been patronised by a coarser type of client — or perhaps the ale was stronger. Before it there was a stair called the Dug Stair because many of the men leaving the inn were unable to walk straight and went down the stair on their hands and knees.

Not far off was the Geelies' Wynd, probably coming from the Gaelic as this lane would be frequently used by the gillies or serving men of the Abbey. Another derivation is thought to be St Giles' Wynd. Here also was an old barn which once housed a Sabbath School and became the schoolhouse of William Meldrum who did some printing on a simple press which he constructed himself in 1819 while he was teacher in the Brucefield Mill School.

Bruce Street was once known by the monks as Colliers' Row and this does not come, as might be imagined, from the passage of coal carts or the homes of miners. In the Gaelic the word col or cool refers to wood or forest, in Celtic it meant worship. On the west side of this street which ran from the Tolbooth to the Millport or Collier Port, there was an old house taken down in 1867. In it a built-up recess was discovered, holding some coins of Edward I and II, James VI and Charles II. After this, for a long time it was referred to as the Coin house.

To anticipate events it might be added in connection with Bruce Street that the first bank in the town was set up here in 1781, by the Bank of Scotland. Mr Dickie was the agent and Mr William Mitchell, teller and accountant. Mr Dickie had other interests — one imagines that the pressure of business was not too great — for in the cellar of a nearby house, he erected a dye mill which was powered by a large dog and called Willie Dickie's Dug mill.

In later times these houses became the property of the Kerr brothers — Robert, James and John. They were appointed agents of the Commercial Bank and in 1823 they added a small two-storey house which was long known as the Commercial Bank.

The mill which gave its name to the port stood close to the port on the east side on the site of a disused spinning-mill. It was a very noisy clattering mill, mentioned in the Abbey register between 1555 and 1610, though there was a mill here as early as 1150. Behind this old mill until 1824 there stood the town's boiling-house where the handspun yarns were boiled and prepared for the winder or weaver. Next to the boiling-house was the Tanyard, once carried on by Alexander Pearson who rented the place in 1775 for an annual payment of £9-15. What was known as the Skinnery was also here, for which the skinner William Morgan paid a rent of £3.

So it seems that Colliers' Row and the Millport surroundings must have been rather malodorous, especially in hot weather.

Apparently the citizens of Dunfermline, busy with the struggle to survive took little interest in the romantic doings of Prince Charles Edward Stewart in his attempts to re-instate his father as king in place of the Hanoverian George. When the Jacobites arrived triumphantly in Edinburgh notice was sent to Dunfermline that the town council would be expected to pay a contribution to the Prince's funds according to the amount of the town's excise. This they were ordered to pay 'upon pain of rebellion' and two Bailies, Adie and Crawford, travelled to Edinburgh and met Mr Murray of Broughton, the Prince's secretary. They were told that the amount payable was eighty pounds sterling and, this having been reported to the Provost and town council, it was decided to consult the craft-deacons and discuss how the money was to be raised. In spite of the calm tone of the Council reports, it is possible to imagine the consternation that would be aroused by such unlawful demands upon 'the common good' and it would be small comfort to be assured that no further levy would be laid upon them for at least six months.

Mr John Knox was delegated to arrange the transaction but there was some delay in collecting the sum involved and such was the impatience of the Prince's followers that the very next day saw the arrival in the town of the Earl of Kellie with some Highlanders to meet the Council and demand the money. Two subsequent extraordinary meetings were held by the Council that day and the next, after which John Knox was appointed to hand over the sum of twenty pounds to Lord Kellie in part payment. It was hoped to delay the rest of the sum till the fate of the rebellion had been decided one way or the other. The Earl of Kellie evidently agreed to this arrangement but in December the Jacobites were back again in the town, demanding the 'toun's cess under pain of military execution'. The Highland soldiers lodged in the town and ten days later the town council was instructing John Knox to pay not only the town's excise but also to give the insurgents 'supply', probably meaning food which was not to exceed sixteen pounds sterling.

After that, of course, the Jacobite army went on to meet its destruction and no doubt the city-fathers breathed a sigh of relief. It seems that they were indeed on the Hanoverian's side for in February 1746 they sent a deputation to wait upon the Duke of Cumberland and congratulate His Royal Highness upon 'his success against the rebels' when the Royal burghs held their annual meeting in Edinburgh.

No doubt the town's finances soon recovered from this unexpected demand upon 'the common good' and after the rebellion was over life settled back into its usual routine. But progress was in the air and things were moving.

A new street was proposed, running downhill from the Market cross and to this end the Council decided to purchase James Legat's tenement and yard. This cost the town 1250 merks Scots and soon afterwards David Wilson's yard to the south of Legat's property was also bought. Two years later in 1754 the thoroughfare, called New Street till 1805 when it became Guildhall Street, was opened to traffic. The town council seems at this time to have got the bit between its teeth as far as public expenditure and modernisation were concerned for next we find them authorising the purchase of six new lamps to be placed to the best advantage in the darker streets. These lamps cost twelve shillings each and were so favourably regarded by the Council that six more were ordered. These shed light upon such corners as the East Port, the Collieraw, the Cross, the Flesh Market tenement, the east end of the Maygate, the Rotten Row, and two men, Robert Meldrum and David Christie were paid annually ten pounds between for looking after the lamps. They also received three pounds of candles.

The town council then turned its attention to the matter of the town-ports which had long been obsolete, with some being in ruins. The East Port and Crosswynd Ports went in 1752, the Mill or Collier Row Port in 1754, but St Catharine's or West Port remained till 1780. It was the oldest port of the town, having been mentioned in a charter of 1327 in connection with St Catharine's chapel and almshouse outside the port. It was a tall narrow building with an archway only seven feet wide and a room which was entered by a door from the churchyard.

Coal carts were banned from 'cawing' coals through any of the streets except the New Row and along Queen Anne Street, then known as the Backside and those who disobeyed this order were fined 'at each back-load' six pennies, each cart-load nine pennies. Notices were placed on all the church doors 'so that none might pretend ignorance'. It is apparently presumed that all colliers and coal merchants were able to read.

Meanwhile there was a war going on across the Atlantic and Sir Peter Halkett, Provost of the town and an officer in the 44th Regiment of Foot was fighting against the French and Indians near Fort du Quesne. Both he and his son James were killed in the encounter and the town council, while observing the town's sorrow at this disaster, had to elect another Provost. Their choice was Alexander Wedderburn who was only twenty-two. He was re-elected twice but as he was by then an advocate he resigned from the Provostship and went to Edinburgh to practise law. Some trouble with a Judge of the Court of Session caused him to go south to London where he became Lord High Chancellor of England and was buried in St Paul's.

He was followed as Provost for the next two years by Sir Francis Halkett of Pitfirrane and then, maybe a sign of the times, a majority vote in the Council elected David Turnbull as Provost.

The town itself was spreading its wings. As well as new streets, new roads were being made, stretching towards Kirkcaldy in the east and North Queensferry to the south by the Spittal Brig. Some of the linen manufacturers, hitherto content to deal with local orders and hawkers, were now sending representatives as far afield as London where they found a ready sale for their wares. There were 260 looms in the town and another three hundred in the district. On the other side of the coin a most unpopular window tax was introduced and the town council, worried by the price of meal and oats, arranged to make a large purchase on behalf of the poorer citizens who were suffering from a malignant fever that lingered in the town for some months.

Then came the death of George II and the accession of George III, and, though these matters really meant little to the citizens, the town council agreed to send a loyal address to the King, by the hands of Mr Haldane, their member of Parliament.

The most important event concerned with Dunfermline at this time was the decision of George Chalmers of Pittencrieff to build a new bridge over the Tower burn, continuing the High Street to the west. This matter is first recorded in the Burgh Records in November 1765 but it was not until May, 1769, that a final arrangement was made. As the Tolbooth or Townhouse had long been in need of extensive and expensive repair, it was thought this to be a good opportunity to take it down, open up a way for the new road and erect a more modern building.

Dunfermline High Street looking towards Townhouse

This Townhouse which stood till 1879, when it was replaced by the present building of curiously confused Scottish and French Gothic styles, seems to have been a modest affair of one storey with four apartments below street-level, which served as accommodation for the resident warder, a black hole for prisoners and storage for holding the town's lamps and brooms. The front of the building, which was oblong in shape and lay east and west, faced north to the new street, with two large windows on either side of the main door where were six small carved stones, representing the town's arms, the figure of St Margaret, crowns, harps and roses as decoration. To the east side were the clerk's offices and in the south-east corner at the top of Kirkgait was a steeple crowned by a weather-cock. At the foot of the steeple there was a door with the royal arms and the date 1768 above it. The steeple was first intended to be covered with copper but the Council found the cost too great and had to be content with slates. The steeple also boasted a new striking clock which began its duties in 1775. In 1792 two more storeys were added to the building, providing accommodation for the Sheriff court and Council room. The third storey was used as a jail.

The building of Bridge Street was begun in 1772, with a long subterranean channel housing the waters of the Tower burn; two years later came the construction of Chalmers Street, Woodhead Street and Pittencrieff Street, joining up the scattered cottages that had formerly been in rather inaccessible country. Later the new west road out of Dunfermline was taken through what came to be known as Urquhart Cut, gun-powder having been used to force a way through the massive rock formation on the steep hill leading to the village of Crossford. Before these operations began the sloping banks of the glen behind the Town house were called the Back-braes.

On the Back-braes and some forty feet down the bank, close to the burn, there stood an old barn, a stable and a byre with a slaughterhouse nearby, reached by the Tolbooth close and other closes in the Kirkgait and the Collier Row. After Bridge Street was constructed there were, for some years, vacant places on either side of the roadway. At the corner of Collier Row a rough stone wall some ten feet high filled the gap and over it hung the branches of a fine pear tree. Almost opposite was another stone wall with more fruit trees climbing above it. This part of the street was the site of a crockery-market on fair days and not far off was the New Inn with good stables at the back of it. There was another Inn at the corner of Chalmers Street with on the opposite side a meeting-house occupied by a section of Baptists. Other people who lived in the street were Mr Angus of the Post Office who constructed a diving-bell and Mr John Wilson who invented various improvements in hand-loom weaving and died in 1820.

But the building of Chalmers Street brought ruin to George Chalmers of Pittencrieff who was made bankrupt by his creditors. He sold the estate and moved to Edinburgh. A large oil-painting of him was paid for by public subscription and hung in the new Townhouse.

The Rhodes Brewery, Gutterside

13
Streets and Wells

In a growing town like Dunfermline the matter of public wells was of great importance and in 1765 the town council was urged on by the citizens to open up some new ones. At the Tron, Maygate, the foot of Ho' Boys' Close, the foot of New Row (Howgate) top of New Row, the Horse-market, now Douglas Street, in East Port and in the New Street (Guildhall Street). Nethertown had four wells — one at the west end, north side of Nethertown, oppostie the Gusset House, one in front of what is now the Dunfermline and West Fife Hospital, one east of Reid Street and one midway between Reid Street and Moodie Street. Sunken draw wells later became pump wells but most of them remained open or partly covered by flagstones so that heavy rain frequently contaminated them with filth and rubbish washed in from the street. In rainy spells the water-channels of these streets, full of deep ruts and hollows, held water stagnant in the summer and overflowing into the wells. Gutterside well was dug into the side of the sharply sloping ground above the Rhodes property. Here the roadway was a few feet above the level of the well and very narrow with a malt-kiln built in 1695 rising above it. St. Leonard's Well had a short 'dog' stair carefully covered over, within the entrance of the road leading to Brucefield from Hospital Hill. It was a shallow, but constant spring, soft and pleasant to the taste, and was never completely dry in summer. Strachan's Well, at the back of the Dam, situated where the Tower burn curved from south to east as it entered Wooers' Alley, had a long staircase.

Strachan's Well had a long and troubled history ending in litigation. In 1763 one Robert Flockhart, mason, feued from Captain Grant of Pittencrieff a small piece of land on which he built a dwelling house. He also enclosed the well and appointed one of his tenants to look after it. This man's name was Strachan and so the well came to be known as Strachan's Well. In 1793, Robert Flockhart's son sold the greater part of his property to George Burt, manufacturer, reserving for himself and his stepmother all rights of entrance to the well. Six years later Mr Burt improved the entrance to the well by building a stair of seventy-two steps, at the cost of £30 to which the neighbours using the well contributed a guinea each. The well was so popular that the steps began to suffer so Mr Burt decided to close the well, strengthen the wall round it and fix a lock to the strong entrance door. This led to a water famine in the neighbourhood as the well was one that was never dry and in 1804 public feeling among the citizens ran strongly enough for them to send a petition to the Sheriff, asserting their right of entry to the well. The matter went on to the Court of Session, continuing there for more than six years, and in the end the feuars and weavers won their case. An Association was formed under the title of 'The Strachan-well Society' with president, secretary, treasurer and committee 'to watch over and clean out the well and guard the public's interest in it.'

That part of the glen was called Harrie Braes, a corruption of Fleury Braes which referred to the wild roses, whins and broom bushes that covered the steep banks. In 1817 the Harrie Brae flax-spinning mill was erected here and was the cause of a lawsuit later between Mr Hunt of Pittencrieff and Mr Rutherford, owner of the mill.

Wells continued to be used till 1850 when pipes, laid in the streets, brought to an increasing number of houses water from Craigluscar Reservoir.

As Dunfermline grew more prosperous so did the citizens improve their appearance and walk about their cobbled lanes and streets in better clothes. Here were well-to-do merchants in blue or grey coats which, unbuttoned, revealed the splendour of their fancy waistcoats. Their shirts were ornamented with ruffles at breast and wrists while large white stiff neckcloths generally covered the whole chin. They wore tight buttoned drab breeches, white stockings and buckled shoes which in wet weather were covered by black spats or half-boots.

No doubt the fashions in the town were behind the times as communications from the outside world were slow but when the merchants' wives learned from the newssheets or the itinerant packman that wigs and cocked hats were out of favour they would see to it that their husbands had their hair powdered in the new style. They themselves swept about in voluminous skirts with three-tiered falls of lace at the elbows of their tight sleeves. But only ladies of fashion who travelled in sedan-chairs or their own coaches to attend balls and plays in Edinburgh would indulge in the deep decolletage that was considered indecent in Presbyterian circles. In winter they wore wide beaver hats and galoshes; in summer slippers with ribbons and small bonnets sometimes decorated with posies of artificial flowers.

At the other end of the social scale old men, passing the evening of their days by the ingle-nook or on a sunny street corner, wore large blue bonnets, hodden-grey coats and loose waistcoats with roomy pockets. Their breeches were of hodden-grey or corduroy and their clumsy shoes were sometimes ornamented with a metal buckle. A five-foot staff each helped them to attend church or market. Their women folk wore plaids over their plain woollen gowns with a mutch or a coal scuttle bonnet on their severely dressed hair.

Walking for everyone was made easier when the cobblestones in the High Street and part of Bridge Street were replaced by plainstanes or pavements. Other less pleasant additions to the streets were the toll-bars which were first erected in 1790 at Limekilns Road, Baldridge burn, Spittal and Town Green. These tolls were small sums collected from everyone who passed the tollgates or toll houses, some of the money going towards the upkeep of roads and bridges with a fixed charge for pedestrians, horseman, a shepherd with sheep or a drover with cattle.

The toll houses provided accommodation for the toll-keeper's family and as the post was put up for auction and went to the highest bidder, there was small chance of anyone slipping past unnoticed. Reconditioned toll houses can still be seen at strategic points near towns or villages, their windows watching the traffic from all directions. They were not entirely abandoned till late in the 19th century.

By 1792 when the population of Dunfermline had risen to five thousand, one hundred and ninety-two there were twelve hundred looms in the town, weaving cottons and linens as well as the famous Dunfermline damask. As the looms were located in the weavers' homes, the streets must have hummed and trembled to the tread of the clumsy machines that, miraculously, produced such delicate designs and fabrics.

Other industries in the town were flourishing — a flour-mill, a tannery, various breweries, another coal-pit sunk at Halbeath, when a steam-engine was erected by the celebrated Patrick Miller and his assistant William Symington. A steelyard was bought by the town council and set up by the flesh-market, near the Cross.

The establishment of a lending library in 1789 with an annual subscription of five shillings, led to the formation of such societies as the Bachelors' Club; the Ancient Society of Weavers became a Friendly Society and for a short period the Friends of the People, a secret political society, indulged in some plotting against the Government. Perhaps it was to counter these activities as well as the threat of the Napoleonic Wars, that the Dunfermline fencibles were raised in 1795. They were known as the Blue Fencibles because of their blue uniforms but in 1798 they joined the Volunteers and wore red coats. One of the most important events of 1799 was the passing of an Act of Parliament by which the miners were at last entirely emancipated, an event which the Dunfermline colliers greeted with great relief. At last they would be able to regard themselves as free men, able to live and work where they chose.

Visitors to Dunfermline included some famous people, such as Thomas Pennant the celebrated traveller and

Adam Smith, the Kirkcaldy philosopher while in 1787 Robert Burns himself arrived to pay his respects to the memory of Robert the Bruce. When he was shown the large flat stone that was mistakenly supposed to be the site of the great King's grave, he knelt down and kissed it. Then in another mood he mounted the pulpit and while his friend sat on the stool of repentance, he gave him such a lecture as he himself had frequently endured from his minister at home.

It seems fitting to close this brief account of Dunfermline in the 18th century with a reference to the Queen's House, the Constables' and Bailie's dwellings by the Abbey. For many years the buildings had been falling into decay and in 1797 Captain Phin of Pittencrieff, owner of the property, sold the materials — stones, slates, worm-eaten wooden beams and floors which had stood there for almost two hundred years. The removal of these ruins must have opened up the neighbourhood and let a breath of fresh air into what had been a crowded corner by the Abbey but it was another part of Dunfermline's heritage and soon these ancient buildings, which had seen pomp and ceremony, music, laughter and in the end the shouts of a crowd watching a cockfight, would be entirely forgotten.

In April 1801 the first Government Census was taken in Dunfermline. This records that the population of the town numbered nine thousand, nine hundred and eighty-seven with seven hundred and five occupied houses. There were also fourteen schools of varying importance and no fewer than ten churches and meeting places — the Auld Kirk, Baptist, Secession Chapel, Relief, Cameronian Tabernacle, Independents, Anti-Burgher and Auld Lichts. Apparently one read one's Bible or listened to a few sermons and made one's choice. No doubt the need for prayers and repentance was urged by all the ministers of whichever persuasion as the town was afflicted by a 'great dearth' which meant increased prices, rationed bread and the establishment of a public food-kitchen to feed the starving. The elements, too, seemed to regard the town with disfavour for a great thunderstorm brought down more of the church ruins and there were earthquake shocks recorded in the summer of

1802, when people ran from their beds into the streets while in the houses crockery was broken and furniture disturbed.

A more cheerful note concerns the visit of the famous violinist Neil Gow and his son, when he played at the grand dinner and ball given in the Townhouse by the members of the Fife Hunt.

There was a bank robbery in November 1801, when, on a stormy night, a house-painter named M'Coull broke into the Bank of Scotland at the west end of Bridge Street and carried off over a hundred pounds. He was never caught and was again successful when, five years later, he murdered William Begbie, porter at the British Linen Company's bank in the Canongate of Edinburgh, who was carrying over a thousand pounds from the Leith branch to the head office. The murder weapon was a pointed blade with soft paper wrapped round the hilt and was plunged into the unfortunate Mr Begbie's heart. A most intensive search was carried out by the authorities and many people were arrested on suspicion but without success. Some months later a roll of banknotes was found, hidden in a cavity of a wall where Drummond Place, Edinburgh, now stands. They proved to be the stolen notes. The end of the story came with the arrest, trial and conviction of M'Coull in 1820 for robbing the Paisley Union Bank in Glasgow and he died in prison a year later. No doubt the law-abiding citizens of Dunfermline would be keenly interested in the details of this unsolved mystery, for M'Coull's guilt regarding the British Linen Bank affair was never really proved though suspicion pointed strongly in his direction.

The threat of a French invasion following the success of Napoleon's campaigns in Europe now gave the city fathers some concern. Recruiting sergeants appeared in the town on market days and in 1804 the Dunfermline Volunteers urgently canvassed for recruits. Drilling went on in the Bowling Green watched by large crowds. Their ranks included such eminent local personages as Provost Moodie (Lieutenant-Colonel) Captain Andrew Adie and Robert Stark of Brucefield, John and James Stenhouse, fish-bearers and William Beveridge, merchant and paymaster. Martial music was provided by a band-drummers, hautboy, cymbals and a bugle.

About this time a beacon-fire on the Borders started the alarm that Napoleon had landed and as beacon after beacon carried the message through the country, the Dunfermline Volunteers, roused at midnight, were preparing to defend the town when news came that it had all been a mistake. No doubt the Volunteers were mustered again to join in the public mourning when the news came of the death of Nelson, reaching the town in November, 1805. It was indeed a national mourning but, in spite of the fact that Admiral Mitchell of the Hill House was now an Admiral of the Blue, the Navy was not very popular with the citizens. There had been several visits made by the Press gang in the past and many of the men thus forcibly taken off to serve in the navy had not returned.

Andrew Mitchell of the Hill had had a long and finally successful career in the navy. After a spell of unemployment in 1799 when he was a rear admiral, he helped to defeat the Dutch in the Texel, was raised to the rank of Vice-Admiral and appointed Commander-in-Chief at Sheerness. In 1800 he presented a set of Dutch flags, taken at the Battle of the Texel, to the Burgh of Dunfermline and soon after this the town council opened a subscription to pay for a full-length painting of the Admiral to hang up in the Town Hall. But the Admiral of the Blue did not enjoy his eminence for long as he died a few months later on February 26th, 1806.

There was no stage-coach connecting Dunfermline with the outside world till 1824. People travelling to Edinburgh or Glasgow or London had to meet the coach at Inverkeithing or Crossgates till in 1806 the innkeeper of the Old Inn, Laurence Millar, began to run a coach called the Fly. It went to Aberdour, the passengers being conveyed by boat to Leith, and was proving popular when his horses were killed in 1807 by the fall of a ruined tower at the south-west corner of the Abbey. This disaster brought the project to a halt and there was no public transport till 1824 when a stage-coach called the Antiquary provided a return service between Dunfermline and Edinburgh every weekday.

There were of course, plenty of private coaches, dog-carts, wagons and sedan-chairs to cater for long or short journeys, though most of the population went on foot, thinking nothing of walking several miles to attend a revivalist meeting or to visit friends. The streets were quiet after dark, though the town council went on providing more and more lamps. These, lit by train-oil and burning cotton wicks, gave out a very poor light and only burned for a few hours before the lamp lighter came round with his ladder and blew them out. In shops there were long or short candles, maybe an oil-lamp or a primitive 'cruisie' which smelt strongly of train-oil. Churches were gloomy places with cords pulling down large circles of candles up and down from the roof with the danger of candle-grease falling down on the congregation's Sunday clothes. Some-times, during the service, most of the candles were extinguished. If citizens had to move through the streets at night, they usually carried a hand-lantern to light their way over the gutters and uneven cobblestones and up dark closes. It must be remembered, too, that even the simple act of lighting a fire meant using a tinder-box to supply the spark which, in its turn, ignited the spunks that were laid under the wood or coal in the fireplace. Spunks were shavings impregnated with sulphur and were sold by spunk-makers who went from door to door with their bundles.

Of course, in those days no-one was in a hurry. The housewives gossiped when they sat at the well, the weavers, if not impelled by actual want, worked what hours they pleased and sometimes went off to indulge in a little illegal fishing or poaching. Shopkeepers joined their customers at the shopdoor and commented on the passing scene. Entertainments could be anticipated for fairs were held on regular dates on ground at the west end of Nethertoun, now Elgin Street. These dates had been granted in some case by Royal warrant. James VI granted two, on the first of March and the Fourteenth of September. Free fairs were also held on the 20th July and the 22nd October, each continuing for three days, while an Act of Parliament, passed in 1701, gave the Magistrates of

Dunfermline permission to hold a fair on the second Wednesday of January. There was a weekly market for butter, cheese and eggs held at the Tron on Fridays and a weekly market at the Cross on Tuesdays when grain samples were laid out.

The coming of a fair must have stirred up some excitement in the town and district, for in the canvas and wooden booths marvellous entertainments were promised with colourful posters tempting folk to spend anything up to sixpence to see the wonders inside. There were also small menageries of wild beasts and a circus ring round which Ord, the famous equestrain would gallop, sometimes astride four or five horses. There were races, too, held in the same district of the town, on horse or on foot, and at certain times of the years, as the nineteenth century advanced, there were the Masonic processions. Freemasons had, of course, been existing in the town since the fourteenth century and had always played an important part in the town's affairs. Now, it seemed, they were becoming even more powerful.

In 1809 the town was threatened by another calamitous fire in Rotten Row and as only buckets and pitchers from the dam and the burn could be found to fight the blaze, the city fathers decided it was time to invest in an efficient fire engine. A year later two fire engines, worked by hand, came to Dunfermline from London and soon after they were installed they were used to put out a fire in Collier Row.

In the same year the town council approved the Provost's suggestions that the names of the streets ought to be put up on corner houses, a proposal which shed some homely light on some of the citizens. Here is a selection — High Street from Cross to Townhouse, from Cross to East Port. East Port Street or Town's End from East Port to Stobies'. Canmore Street from Mr. White's to Mr George Spence's. Maygate from Mrs Black to Mr Gibb's, Kirkgait. Collier Row from Provost Wilson's to the Dam. Bridge Street from Townhouse to Rutherford's Corner. Chalmers Street from Mr Rutherford's corner to Mr M'Robbie's. Knabbie Street from the Low Dam to the Slaughterhouse.

Rotten Row from opposite Provost Moodie's entry to the turning to the chapel kirk.

It had also been decided to add a steeple to the Townhouse which meant the expenditure of sixty pounds and while they were about it, the Guildhall was provided

Dunfermline Abbey

with a spire which gave the building its title when in 1817 it became the Spire Hotel. This building activity also included the restoration of the old tower on the south-west corner of the Abbey, in which an effort was made by a local architect to retain some resemblance to the original tower.

In 1811 another census was taken of the town's population which discovered that this was 6,492 in the town and suburbs, 11,649 in burgh and parish which meant there had been a considerable increase in both burgh and parish. In the same year an Act of Parliament was passed for the paving, lighting, cleaning, widening and otherwise improving the streets. This entailed choosing commissioners and officers who were to superintend every municipal activity from removing old houses, planning new ones, watching over drains, bleaching-greens, public-wells to keeping an eye on 'the Magistrates and the Proprietors of alehouses.'

The new boundaries of the burgh were laid out in detail together with the grounds and tenements, the houses, gardens and yards. Special estates and mansions were enumerated such as Briery Hill, Rhodes, Eliot's Hill, the Spittal and Hospital of St. Leonard's. The town was also divided into wards and in this again the names of various citizens came into prominence as the extent of each ward was noted. Such as in the Second District or Ward which commenced 'at the West End of the High Street from a house in which lived Barbara Adie, widow, on the south and that on the north side now occupied by James Russell, writer, to include South Chapel Street and the lanes and closes on both sides and to terminate at the Cross, at and including the house of David Black, town-clerk, on the south and William Buchan, merchant, on the north. For which Ward two commissioners were to be elected.'

There were ten wards in the town and the description, though too long to be included here, as given in Henderson's Annals, is of great interest for those with any knowledge of the town's topography.

During the first years of the nineteenth century, Dunfermline, while steadily increasing in wealth and import- ance, continued to be largely cut off from easy communication with the outside world. Ferries across the Forth were still at the mercy of wind and tide and only the stagecoach roads were kept in good repair. Of course sons and fathers went off to fight in the wars against Napoleon, many did not return or came back, maimed, to drag their wooden legs across an inn's doorstep and relate hair-raising tales of what had gone on over the battlefields in Spain. There could have been no feeling of prospective victory in the air but the whole affair must have seemed very far away and no doubt folk turned with relief to discussing the wonderful achievement of Henry Meldrum who had successfuly woven a seamless shirt on his loom.

There were other interests too — the little railway that carried coal between Dunfermline and Charlestown, and from Venturefair to Knabbie Row, societies that were formed, like the Burns Club and the Shoemakers' Society, the Friendly Societies of the Maltmen and the Whipmen, The Commercial Bank opened a branch that closed a few years later to be re-established in 1823, while a branch of the Bank of Scotland was opened in Guildhall Street with the Provost David Wilson and William Beveridge appointed joint-agents. A Tradesman's Library at 60 High Street was formed in 1818 and John Miller opened a circulating library in his High Street Bookshop. In this connection it is interesting to note that in 1810 Davie Paton began printing on a home-made printing-press and dealt with songs, small books, advertisements and funeral announcements. One of these small books, published in 1812, was 'A Dialogue betwixt the Old and New Burgar Kirk of Dunfermline, overheard by a benighted Traveller, to which is added An Elegee on the Much-lamented Death of the Rev. Mr Campbell. A.M. 1811'. Mr Paton's printing seems to have been as individual as his spelling.

Other printing-presses in the town were run by John Millar and Andrew Angus, while David Paton and James Lothian owned private presses and produced some interesting literature regarding Dunfermline's history, both real and imaginary sometimes in rhyme and local dialect. One of the most important published in 1815 was that written by John Fernie, one of the ministers of the Abbey Church, who lived in the last house at the east end of Canmore Street on the south side. It is a small book, containing copperplate engravings of various views of the town and many interesting details about the town's past and present character, with table of statistics regarding coal, corn, population and trades. Mr Fernie succeeded his father, Thomas Fernie, who came to the town after being chaplain in the army, and occupied the Abbey pulpit for forty-four years, dying at the advanced age of ninety-two. Mr John Fernie did not enjoy the same robust health as his father and did not live long enough to realise the continuing success of his little book, as he died a year after its publication. The meagre amount of his stipend may have had something to do with this. There was at that time no manse or glebe attached to the Abbeychurch and to make up for this deficiency, as many ministers grew crops on their land, the senior minister was paid £3-6-8, the junior £1-13-4, per annum, with about nineteen chalders of victual, half-meal and half-barley, and £1-10 to pay for the communion wine and the bread.

It is pleasant, however, to reflect that Mr Fernie would have learnt of the final defeat of Napoleon in 1815. The news was greeted with great public rejoicing, cheering crowds in the streets, illuminations soaring up into the June night. The war, that had been going on for years and years, had now at last come to an end. Surviving sons and husbands would come home to settle down to the loom or the plough, war widows would remarry and more children would be born for John Fernie's successors to baptise. As if to celebrate and anticipate the future, the new Grammar school was finished in 1817 and opened to the pupils who had been, during the building of it accommodated in the lower flat of the Townhouse. This school stood on the north side of Queen Anne Street, on the site of the present Post Office. It was a substantial building with a tower that contained the stair leading up to the headmaster's quarters. Above the main-door was a carving of the Burgh Arms, cut in stone together with the inscriptions 'Fave mini mi Deus 1625. Reconditum 1816. D. Wilson Prefecto.' Sculptured stones that had decorated the former school were built into the walls and there were spaces for a clock and a schoolbell housed in a small turret.

It may have been the successful completion of this project that turned the city fathers' attention to the building of a new Abbey church which led, in turn, to the opening of a most important chapter in the history of Dunfermline.

Dunfermline High Street, 1920

14
Bruce's Tomb

After the collapse of the central tower of the Abbey it was decided that the new church should be erected on the site of the eastern part of the church which, disused for two hundred years was now in ruins. A great deal of excavation had to be done and the authorities were naturally interested to find what might lie beneath the great stones of the Choir. It was known that many Royal tombs lay in this area so no-one was surprised when, on the 17th February 1818, the workmen came on a vault by the side of the high altar. But there was a sudden wave of excitement when, on further exploration, the men in charge of the excavations became convinced that they had found the long-lost tomb of King Robert the Bruce.

Under the covering stones with their crumbling iron rings a smaller vault was discovered, seven feet long. In this inner vault lay the skeleton of a man about six feet tall, wrapped in two thin sheets of lead through which protruded the bones of knees, feet and breast. There had evidently been a shroud of cloth-of-gold and round the body were pieces of oak which had once formed the handsome coffin. There was little doubt from the size and evident importance of the skeleton that these were indeed the remains of the great King and, while the vault was closed and watched over day and night by constables of the burgh, the news was sent to the Barons of the Exchequer. They ordered large flat stones to be placed over the vault, secured by iron bars, till some decision could be made about a more thorough investigation.

It was very necessary to guard this area as the laying of the foundation-stone only a few days later on the tenth of March, brought crowds to the churchyard to witness the ceremony. Everywhere work was at a standstill as smiths, weavers, tradesmen of every sort closed their premises and flocked to the neighbourhood of the Town hall, perhaps to join in one of the processions that assembled there or to play in a band or wave a Masonic flag.

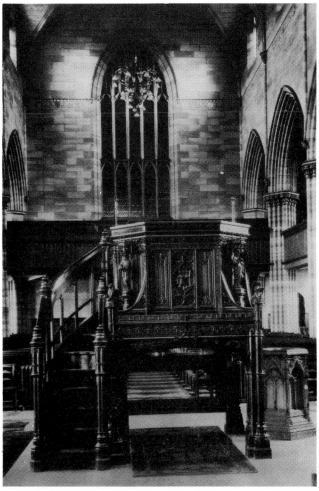

Pulpit and Tomb of Robert the Bruce, Dunfermline Abbey

At a quarter to three the principal procession set out from the Townhouse for the short march down the Kirkgait to the Abbey churchyard. First came a band, playing the Masons' anthem, followed by the Brethren of St John and two men carrying the helmet and sword of Robert the Bruce, lent for the occasion by the Earl of Elgin who had his place in the procession after the architects and contractors of the new church. Dressed in uniform the Earl was accompanied by the Provost. Then came the two beadles of the parish, the Rev. Mr M'Clean and Rev. Mr Peter Chalmers in their gowns and bands as collegiate ministers of the parish, Lord Bruce, Sir Charles Halkett of Pitfirrane, Mr Hunt of Pittencrieff, magistrates of the burgh, members of the Presbytery, the Kirk session, the town council and many of the more eminent citizens.

The foundation ceremony seems to have followed the usual routine. A bottle encased in lead, containing four rolls of parchment and copies of the London Courier and the Morning Chronicle, together with several coins of the realm, was placed in the prepared cavity. Corn, oil and wine were poured over all this while his lordship uttered the Masonic benediction. Then there was a prayer from Mr M'Clean and what must have been a very long address from the Earl. However, the tedium of this was relieved by the Earl breaking into song — the first stanza of 'Scots Wha Hae' which was warmly received by the crowd, estimated at about ten thousand. David Wilson, the Provost, replied to the Earl and the processions returned to the Townhouse where, by special permission of the Earl, the sword and helmet of Bruce were waved aloft and the band played 'Scots Wha Hae to the great and noisy satisfaction of the crowd.'

There was no further examination of the royal remains till November 1819. By that time the walls of the new church had been built to a height of seven feet so that it was possible to shut off the site and keep away unwelcome sightseers. The opening of the tomb was attended by the Barons of the Exchequer in the persons of the Lord Chief Baron and Mr Clark Rattray, together with such eminent scientists as Sir Henry Jardine, Dr Gregory, His Majesty's

First Physician in Scotland, Dr Munro, Professor of Anatomy at Edinburgh University, Mr W. Burn, architect of the new church, the ministers and magistrates. Many of the local landowners and heritors of the Abbey church added to the muster of those who watched the disinterment of the royal remains.

From comments and notes taken at the time, it seems that the greatest impression was made by the size and strength of Bruce's jawbone, which had been fractured at some time. Only a few of his upper teeth were missing and as proof positive of his identity, the breast-bone had been sawed through from end to end, so that the heart which James Douglas was to take on his crusade could be removed. The skull was entire and Dr Gregory, who seems to have been a man of some spirit, jumped down into the trench that had been dug all round the stone grave and held it up for the spectators to see.

'This,' he exclaimed, 'is the head of King Robert!'

The scientists made various other inspections, noting how some of the cartileges, together with tendons and ligaments, had melted into dust, and it was with the idea of preserving the skeleton from further decay that they decided to pour melted pitch into the new leaden coffin that had been provided for the re-burial. The bones of the skeleton were carefully replaced, wrapped in the original lead covering before the melted pitch was added. For some curious reason, various books and articles contained in leaden boxes were laid in the pitch before the coffin-lid went on top. The books were Barbour's *Life of Bruce*, Lord Hailes' *Annals of Scotland*, Kerr's *History of King Robert's Reign*, Fernie's *History of Dunfermline*, the *Edinburgh Almanack*, and some current Edinburgh newspapers. Gold and silver coins of the reign of George from 1787 to 1819 went in too.

Previous to the re-interment, the skeleton, lying upon a wooden board on top of the coffin, was shown to the crowds that came to Dunfermline from all parts of Scotland. Moving in a long, hushed procession through the new church, they passed the vault and looked wonderingly at the King whose body had lain unrecognised in its gold-threaded shroud for four hundred and eighty-nine years.

Finally the vault was levelled to the floor and upon the top bricks set in mortar were placed, on which, in the exact situation where the body was found, the leaden coffin was laid, filled nearly to the top with melted pitch, and the top soldered on, with the following inscription — King Robert Bruce — 1329-1819.

For some reason best known to themselves the authorities chose to blazon the name of King Robert the Bruce in large stone letters on the church-tower, thankfully indecipherable from a distance. One of the parchment rolls interred at the foundation ceremony contained a long and fulsome account of his life, but I prefer to end this short account of my native town's history with part of the epitaph by Fordoun, which was probably inscribed on the panels of his tomb.

'HE LED THE KINGDOM OF THE SCOTS TO FREEDOM BY HIS UPRIGHTNESS. NOW LET HIM LIVE IN THE CITADEL OF HEAVEN.'

Chronology

Rulers of Scotland (Regnum dates) 1005-1707 and Great
Britain 1707-1901)

Kings and Queen

Malcolm II	March 1005
Duncan I	November 1034
Macbeth	August 1040
Lulach	August 1057
Malcolm III, son of Duncan I	March 1058
Donal Bain	November 1093
Duncan II, son of Malcolm III	May 1094
Donal Bain with nephew Edmund	November 1094
Edgar, son of Malcolm III	October 1097
Alexander, brother of Edgar	January 1107
David I, brother to Edgar and Alexander	April 1124
Malcolm IV, grandson	May 1153
William I, brother	December 1165
Alexander II, son	December 1214
Alexander III, son	July 1249
Margaret, daughter of King Erik II of Norway	March 1286

Throne in dispute — 13 claimants during the period September 1290-
November 1292
John Balliol, great-great-great grandson
of David I, awarded the throne by Edward I
of England. Later deposed by him.   Nov 1292
Interregnum and intermittent war with England — government entrusted to
John de Warenne, Earl of Surrey and Hugh Cressingham.
William Wallace   Insurrection 1297-1298
Between 1296 and 1306 there were a series of Scottish Guardians and English
Lieutenants with responsibility for Scotland.

Kings and Queen

Robert I (Bruce)	March 1306
David II, son	June 1329-Feb 1371

Robert II, nephew Robert I	Feb 1371
Robert III, son	April 1390
James I, son	April 1406
James II, son	Feb 1437
James III, son	August 1460
James IV, son	June 1488-Sept 1513
James V, son,	Sept 1513-1542
Mary, daughter	Dec 1542-July 1567
James VI, son, became James I of England from March 1603	
	July 1567-Mar 1625
Charles I, son	Mar 1625

Lord Protectors

Oliver Cromwell	1653
Richard Cromwell, son	1658-1659

Kings and Queens

Charles II, son of Charles I	May 1660
James VII, also James II of England	Feb 1685-Dec 1688
William III of Orange with Mary II, daughter of James VII	1689-Mar 1702
Anne, sister of Mary II	Mar 1702-Aug 1714

1 May 1707 — Scotland united with England and Ireland as the Kingdom of Great Britain and Ireland

Kings and Queens (House of Hanover)

George I, great-grandson of James VI and I	1714-1727
George II, son	1727-1760
George III, son	1760-1820
George IV, son	1820-1830
William IV, brother	1830-1837
Victoria, niece	1837-1901

Index